A Kid's Guide to the Names of God

TONY EVANS

HARVEST HOUSE PUBLISHERS
EUGENE, OREGON

Unless otherwise indicated, all Scripture quotations are taken from the New American Standard Bible®, © 1960, 1962, 1963, 1968, 1971, 1972, 1973, 1975, 1977, 1995 by The Lockman Foundation. Used by permission. (www.Lockman.org)

Verses marked NIV are taken from the Holy Bible, New International Version®, NIV®. Copyright © 1973, 1978, 1984, 2011 by Biblica, Inc.® Used by permission. All rights reserved worldwide.

Cover illustration by Krieg Barrie

Cover design by Left Coast Design

Interior design by Chad Dougherty

HARVEST KIDS is a registered trademark of The Hawkins Children's LLC. Harvest House Publishers, Inc., is the exclusive licensee of the federally registered trademark HARVEST KIDS.

A KID'S GUIDE TO THE NAMES OF GOD

Copyright © 2017 Tony Evans

Published by Harvest House Publishers
Eugene, Oregon 97402
www.harvesthousepublishers.com

ISBN 978-0-7369-6961-1 (pbk.)
ISBN 978-0-7369-6962-8 (ebook)

All rights reserved. No part of this publication may be reproduced, stored in a retrieval system, or transmitted in any form or by any means—electronic, mechanical, digital, photocopy, recording, or any other—except for brief quotations in printed reviews, without the prior permission of the publisher.

Printed in the United States of America

22 23 24 25 / BP-CD / 10 9 8 7 6 5

Contents

So Many Names!

When someone asks you, "What's your name?" you usually respond by saying your first name, right? Jacob. Elizabeth. Devon. Maddie. Aaron. But you have other names too. Like your middle name. Or your last name. You also probably have at least one nickname. And if you do stuff online, you have a user name or a screen name—something you chose to reflect who you are. It could be Gymnasticsgirl123 or Pianoguy1. So many names!

When someone gets to know you, they get to know all your names—not just your first name. And if they know you really well, they might even give you a fun nickname. We connect with each other through our names. And when someone uses your name, it makes you feel special—you feel known and important.

It's important to learn the names of other people—our classmates, our teachers, our neighbors. And it's also important to learn the names of God. Wait—what? God has more than one name? Actually, God has a whole bunch of names! He wants us to learn about His names because that helps us get to know Him better. It also helps us connect with Him and grow closer to Him.

Getting to know God by His names is more than simply learning a new word for "God" or figuring out how to pronounce a title He uses. Learning to know God by His names helps us figure out who He is and to experience His awesome power. It's a really terrific way to get to know the Creator of the universe on a more personal level.

Your parents might have named you after a relative or chosen your name just because they really liked how it sounds. Those are both great reasons to be given a name, but in the Bible, people were named for a different reason. Names had a lot of meaning attached to them back then. In fact, Scripture often mentions God Himself changing someone's name to show that something important happened.

For example, Abram means "exalted father," but when God promised Abram he would have many descendants, God changed his name to Abraham, which means "father of a multitude." Jacob, whose name means "deceiver," received a new name after wrestling with God. His new name, Israel, means "one who prevails." And in the New Testament, when Jesus told His disciples He would build His church on a solid foundation, He changed Simon's name to Peter, which means "rock."

One time, when Jesus was praying to the Father, He said, "I have made Your name known to them, and will make it known" (John 17:26). And by "name," Jesus wasn't just talking about letters put together to spell a word. He was explaining that God's heart, mind, will, character, and being—all that God is—would be revealed through His name.

God's names also affect how we interact with Him. We can use one of His names when we're scared, another when we're praising Him, and yet another when we're sick and asking Him for healing. Did you know that God has a name for every situation we find ourselves in? He does!

Now, our own names don't necessarily mean a lot. A child might have the name of a famous person—like Michael Phelps or Taylor Swift—but not be a fast swimmer or a talented singer. The name alone contains no special power. Yet when that name *is* connected to the quality it represents, the result is powerful. And that's the deal with God's names—they all have power. Also, God is so amazing and awesome and incredible that one name alone can't fully tell us all we need to know about Him.

I'm completely convinced that God wants nothing more than for us to truly know Him. And we get to know Him better by knowing His names—what they mean, when we should use them, and why they're so important. Throughout the Bible, when God revealed Himself to His people in a new way, He often revealed a new name.

Here's a great example of this. When God asked Moses to lead the Israelites out of a difficult and challenging situation, He empowered Moses by revealing one of His names. "Moses said to God, 'Behold, I am going to the sons of Israel, and I will say to them, "The God of your fathers has sent me to you." Now they may say to me, "What is His name?" What shall I say to them?'" (Exodus 3:13). In this situation, Moses needed to know God's name. He knew that God's power and authority were attached to His name—and that the Israelites would pay way more attention than if Moses had used his own name. (In chapter 2, we'll see God's response to Moses.)

God had a name for Moses to use to show the Israelites His power, and God has a name for you to use in whatever situation you're facing—fear, friendship troubles, school stress, sickness, worry, or whatever. No matter what name you use, God is always there for you—and you can get to know Him better and better as you learn more of His names and understand how they teach you different things about His character.

Don't worry if this seems a little bit complicated. With God's help, you've got this! In fact, in the New Testament, Jesus tells us that God often reveals His awesomeness, excellence, and splendor to those who have childlike hearts: "I praise You, Father, Lord of heaven and earth, that You have hidden these things from the wise and intelligent and have revealed them to infants" (Matthew 11:25).

Now, if God is willing and able to reveal Himself to babies, He will undoubtedly reveal Himself to you. All it takes is your willingness to learn. And a great way to start learning more about God—who He is, what He does, and how He cares for you—is to learn some of His names.

A big thing to remember is that God's name—no matter which one we're using—is "hallowed," which is another word for holy. We're not supposed to mix up His name with anyone else's name or toss it out lightly. All of God's names are holy, so we are to honor them, respect them, and treat them with reverence.

Here's a good way to look at this. If the president of the United States or the governor of your state were to walk into a room, you wouldn't address him or her by his or her first name. The position demands a certain level of recognition. You wouldn't say, "Hey, dude, what's up?" You would place the title in front of the name and speak it with respect.

God is to be treated with more respect than we would show to anyone else. He is the one and only true God, and we need to treat Him accordingly. This isn't to say that God is mean or scary. He's not. He wants the best for us, and He wants to walk alongside us as we go through life. But He is God, and we always need to remember that. When God isn't treated as He rightfully should be treated, He doesn't take that lightly. And that will affect your relationship with Him.

It's hard to really know God without knowing and understanding some of His names. Have you ever felt as if someone was trying to judge you—to tell you who you are (or tell other people who you are) without truly getting to know you first? A lot of people try to do this with God, but it doesn't work. Why not? Because they don't actually know Him personally.

The better you understand God's names, the more you will worship Him. And by learning several of His names, you'll come to know Him in new ways as He shows up in your life to guide you and direct you and challenge you and love you.

When we know God's names—and honor them and experience the power they represent—we get to know Him better. We see His power working in our lives. We are tuned in to Him, so we notice the amazing things He does for us. And we start sharing His love with others.

Learning God's names together will be exciting! Get ready to discover God in ways you've never imagined and to get to know and experience Him through His powerful and amazing names.

GOD PROVIDES FOR ME!

God is active in your life right now. Even if you can't see Him—like you see your mom or your brother or your cat—He's there. Write down your responses to these questions, and as you do, imagine seeing God right there in your everyday life.

- What did you see or hear (or even smell!) when you woke up this morning and looked around your room and outside?

  ___

  ___

  ___

- What did you eat today?

  ___

  ___

  ___

- What clothing did you wear today?

  ___

  ___

  ___

  ___

- What are some things you did for exercise today? (Think about exercising your brain as well as your body!)

____

____

____

____

- Who did you talk to and laugh with today?

____

____

____

____

Remember, God is right there with you today—everywhere you go and in everything you do.

Elohim

The Strong Creator God

If I say Starbucks, what comes to mind? (Coffee, right?) What about Speedo? (Swimming!) Apple? (Computers and technology.) Gatorade? (Sports drinks.) Levi's? (Jeans.) When a brand name is totally familiar, it's easy to get a mental image of the product.

It's kind of the same thing with the names of God once you get to know them. If course, God isn't selling you a phone or a drink or clothing. He wants you to become familiar with His names because that's one of the best ways to get to know Him better and experience all He has to offer you—which is way better than coffee or even a new computer!

Your brand is your identity. It includes your reputation—what others think about you. When people refer to the Apple brand, they're not talking about an apple with a bite taken out of it. They're talking about what the Apple company stands for—high-quality and innovative electronic devices, like phones and tablets and computers. As we get to know God by discovering His names in Scripture, we see that He has branded His names. They're not just words. Each of those names carries a lot of meaning.

God's names matter! Attached to each one is a set of character qualities, promises, and meanings. And when you know about these things, you discover more of the awesome things He has in store for you.

So let's get straight to the very first name God reveals to us in Scripture—Elohim. We find this name in the first verse of the Bible: "In the beginning God [Elohim] created the heavens and the earth" (Genesis 1:1).

When you introduce yourself to someone, the first thing you tell them about yourself is your first name. It's the main thing you want someone to know about you—the one thing that will make them feel like they know you right away. Same deal with God. It's as if in this verse, He's telling us, "Hello, I'm Elohim." And that name—Elohim—means "Creator." It's the first impression He wants us to have of Him.

FIRST IMPRESSIONS

First impressions are often lasting impressions. Sometimes our first impression—what we think right away when we meet someone—is right, but sometimes it's wrong. Either way, it's usually lasting, especially if we don't continue getting to know the person.

- What were some of your first impressions of your best friend?

____

____

- Which of these first impressions were right, and which were wrong?

____

____

- What would you want someone's first impressions of you to be?

____

____

- What can you do or say so someone will have a correct first impression of you?

____

____

- When you think of God's creation, what's your first impression of Him ?

____

____

One of the main reasons God introduces Himself to us as Elohim, the strong Creator God, is that He wants us to know He's distinct—or separate—from His creation. God is not a tree or a river or a butterfly. He created trees and rivers and butterflies, but He is above and outside of His creation. It's like when you create a painting or construct something out of Legos. You aren't the painting or the Lego creation—even though those things reflect who you are. You are their creator. You're the one who thought up the idea and painted the picture or put the Legos together.

Here, There, and Everywhere!

Another reason God introduces Himself to us as Elohim is to let us know that He is set apart from our ideas of time and space. This can get a little bit confusing, but what's important to remember is that God created everything. And that includes time. So when the Bible says, "In the beginning God created," it must mean that God created the beginning. And that God created time. And—hang with me here!—that if time didn't begin until He created it, then He must have existed before it.

That's a big, brain-stretching idea, isn't it? Think for a minute about the idea of eternity.

- What does the word "eternity" mean to you?

____

____

____

____

- We think in terms of what happened yesterday, today, and tomorrow. What happened to you yesterday?

____

____

- What's going on today?

____

____

- What do you have planned for tomorrow?

____

____

For God, it's a little bit different—a lot different, actually. God doesn't have a yesterday or a tomorrow. That's because He exists outside of our idea of time. Everything for God is *right now* because He has no past and no future. He's eternal—or always. He is the right-now, ever-present God. Which is really comforting to know. He's always there—always has been, always will be. Forever.

When we get to heaven, we'll understand this better. (Whew!) But for now, it's nice to know that God is always with us, no matter where we are. So that's the "time" part. Now about the "space" part.

You and I know and experience only the heavens and the earth. There's a lot to our heavens and earth—the oceans and mountains, moon and stars, rain forests and deserts. Yet the Creator God—Elohim—is beyond all this. He is here, there, and everywhere. He created the heavens and the earth, existing outside of it. But He also fills the heavens and the earth, existing in it. He is everywhere. The word used to describe this is "omnipresent"—everywhere-present at the same time.

God is here, yet He is also there. Elohim—our Creator—is here, there, and everywhere at the same time. No wonder our world is so amazing—it was made by such an amazing Creator!

Take It Personally

With all of this talk about God being here, there, and everywhere, we might be tempted to think of Him as an energy source. Yet the name Elohim doesn't mean God is like that. The Bible would never say, "May the force be with you." God isn't a sci-fi character. He's not a robot that's hard to figure out. He's not an otherworldly being that we just need to accept and be amazed at—as in, "I could never get to know a God like that." Not at all.

Yes, God is amazing, but what's even more amazing is that He wants you to learn about Him and know Him. He's not just a supersmart energy source; He's your personal Creator.

When we read Genesis 1—the first chapter of the first book of the Bible—we see His name Elohim associated with some very personal characteristics:

> Then God [Elohim] said, "Let there be light"; and there was light. God saw that the light was good; and God separated the light from the darkness.

> God called the light day, and the darkness He called night (verses 3-5).

Look back at those verses and see if you can find the verbs—the things that God did. (Hint: There are four words, and one of them is used twice.) Write them down here.

____

____

God said. God saw. God separated. And God called. Each of these actions clearly shows how God is personally involved with His creation. He's not merely a spirit floating around in never-never land. Yes, He exists outside of our ideas of time and space (that brain-stretching idea again!), but He is also actively connected to His creation—to our world and to *us*. If we read ahead a little bit in Genesis, we find God walking with Adam and Eve in the Garden of Eden, hanging out with them in the cool of the day and talking to them (Genesis 3:8-9).

So if we refer to God as an energy, a concept, a force, or an idea, we are not referring to Elohim. As Elohim, God personally interacts with His creation. Yes, God is an amazing Creator, but He is also a personal God who walks with us and talks with us. How awesome is that!

Creativity

God identifies Himself as Elohim 35 times at the start of Scripture. In fact, Elohim is the only name used for God from Genesis 1:1 to Genesis 2:3. Other names come later as God reveals more about Himself throughout His Word, but Elohim is emphasized in the beginning.

All names have a literal translation—an actual meaning. Do you know what your name means? (If you don't, look it up or ask your parents.) Do you think your name fits you? Why or why not?

God's names always fit Him. I believe that God first introduces Himself to us as Elohim, the strong Creator God, because He wants us to understand His power. The literal translation—or actual meaning—of the name Elohim is "strong one." It has to do with His power, and that includes His power to create. The Bible uses the term "created" only when talking about God—never when talking about others. This is because only God has the ability to create something out of nothing. He has the ultimate creativity!

People can make incredible things, but only God has the ability to create something from nothing at all. Think about some different ways you can be creative. What are some things you can make?

Now, write down the materials or ingredients or resources you need to make these things.

If you're knitting a scarf, you need yarn and knitting needles, right? (And the knitting needles are made of metal or plastic, and someone needed fiber and dye to make the yarn.) If you're baking a cake, you need flour, eggs, sugar, and other ingredients. If you're building a bookshelf, you need wood and nails as well as a hammer and saw. Everything comes from something!

Anyone who designs, builds, or creates anything uses something in order to do that. Only God—Elohim—can make something out of nothing. Our own creativity has nothing on His! And want to know something else crazy? God didn't even need to use His hands to create—His mouth was enough. Genesis 1 says that all God had to do was speak the world into existence. Wow!

So God is not only a beyond-talented Creator, He's also capable of doing absolutely anything. In Luke 1:37, when the angel Gabriel tells Mary she will give birth to the Son of God, he adds, "Nothing will be impossible with God."

Sometimes when we're having problems—whether we're frustrated with our homework or upset that our grandparent is in the hospital or scared that our mom can't find a job—we try to fix the problems ourselves. We attempt to create our own solutions without turning to God first. But we need to first remember that Elohim, our strong Creator God, can make something out of nothing. He's done it before, and He continues to do it to this day. He can create an entire world and universe, and He can create the answers to our problems. In fact, He already knows how He's going to take us through them. So we just need to have faith that He will get us there.

All-knowing. All-powerful. Ever-present. Beyond creative. That's our God.

In His Image

Want to know something else mind-blowing? Elohim, the strong Creator God, made us in His image. He did this because He wants us to reflect Him—His goodness, His glory, His strength, His power, and His love. Genesis 1:26 tells us one of our main purposes in life: "God said, 'Let Us make man in Our image, according to Our likeness.'" An image is what you see in a mirror. In the morning when you go to the mirror to get ready for your day, your image flashes back at you from the mirror. It reflects you accurately.

When God made us in His image, He put us at a higher level than all the rest of His creation. He didn't make the flowers in His image. He didn't create the animals in His image. He didn't set the moon and stars in the sky as His image. Only *people* were given this great and awesome privilege. Every other created thing testifies to God's majesty, but only people mirror Him. And this is why we can have such a personal connection with our Creator.

The Bible says, "We are His workmanship, created in Christ Jesus for good works, which God prepared beforehand so that we would walk in them" (Ephesians 2:10). This means that whatever God is going to do for you, He has already done. Whatever God wants you to do, He has already planned it out. Whatever you discover to be the purpose for your life, He has already purposed it.

Your job isn't to try to figure out the map of your life—where you're going to go, what you're going to do, or who you're going to be. God has already drawn the map of your life, and it's a *good* life. And by the way, don't freak out about this! If you really, really want to be a teacher or a scientist or a mom, there's a good chance that God has put that desire in your heart. This doesn't mean that things can't change, but He is never going to force you to do something if you're tuned in to Him.

You don't need to create your future. Elohim, the Creator God, has already created it. You can sleep peacefully at night because you are God's beloved and He is the Creator of all good things. Elohim can make something out of nothing. His creation is wonderful—it's beyond amazing. His is a great name because He is Elohim, the great and powerful Creator.

REMEMBER IT!

"Elohim" starts like "elephant." An elephant is a pretty incredible creation, isn't it? Its massive size, its big floppy ears and long trunk, its powerful walk...But elephants are also loving animals—and actually pretty cute. I'm not saying that God looks like an elephant, but elephants are part of His amazing creation. And if the word "elephant" helps you think of Elohim—the strong Creator God—then go with it!

Can you think of any other ways to remember Elohim, the name God uses to remind us He is the strong Creator God? Write them down here.

____

____

____

____

Jehovah

The Relational God

One day a little boy in school was drawing a picture. His teacher asked him, "What are you drawing?" The young artist answered right away, "I'm drawing a picture of God."

"A picture of God?" she said. "You can't draw a picture of God. No one knows what God looks like."

To which the little boy replied, "Well, they will when I'm done."

Everyone has their own idea of what God looks like. If I were to hand each kid reading this book a piece of paper and say, "Draw what you think God looks like," no two pictures would look the same. (You can try this with your family or friends! Don't show each other your drawings until you're done—then compare.)

It's impossible to completely know what God is really like, and that's because God is so incredible that we can't comprehend His goodness and His love and His power. But God has given us hints—a whole bunch of them—that show us who He is. Better than that, He knows us and longs for us to know Him.

Just for fun, why don't you use the space below to make your own drawing that reflects what you know about God right now? You can actually draw a picture or make a list of words or write a poem—whatever you choose!

When you're done with this book, you can turn back and look at your picture or list or poem. And you can see how much you've discovered about who God is by learning some of His names and what they mean.

As we read further into the Bible, we soon come in contact with a name of God that you might have heard in Sunday school lessons or in songs you sing in church. It's also the name for God that is used most frequently in the Old Testament. We might think of it as God's most familiar name. This name is Jehovah.

Attention, Please!

One of the best ways to learn something is through storytelling. And we're going to learn more about God's name Jehovah through the true story of Moses.

Do you remember much about the life of Moses in the Bible—who he was and the things he did? Take a few minutes to scribble down anything you remember about Moses.

____

____

____

____

You might remember Moses as a baby (which is a super great story, by the way!), but we're going to meet up with Moses when he was a lot older. At this point in his life, God had promised Moses a great future, but Moses was feeling really insecure and down on himself. He had done something really bad—he had killed a man. And to hide this bad thing he'd done, he had escaped to the desert and become a shepherd.

Maybe Moses thought he could hide from God there. But you can never run away from God. He cares too much about you, and He will always find you and help you receive His love and forgiveness.

There in the desert, God revealed Himself to Moses in the form of a burning bush. Now, a bush that was on fire but that never burned up—that would get your attention, wouldn't it? And God in the middle of a burning bush? Well, that would totally make you stop and look! And what Moses saw and heard was that God had a plan for him. That plan was to lead the Israelites out of slavery in Egypt. But Moses freaked out. No way could he do this! He was content just to hide out in the desert—a bearded dude and his sheep.

This is the point in the story when we're introduced to the name of God we're looking at in this chapter—Jehovah. Moses asks God, "Okay, God, so You want me to go down and tell Pharaoh he's supposed to let Your people go. I get that. But when I do, people are going to start asking me a lot of questions, like 'Who suddenly made you boss?'"

Have you ever felt as if you couldn't do anything right? Have you ever felt completely unsure of yourself when other people were counting on you? Not a good feeling! That's how Moses felt.

This is when God tells Moses another one of His names.

> God said to Moses, "I AM WHO I AM. This is what you are to say to the Israelites: 'I AM has sent me to you.'"
>
> God also said to Moses, "Say to the Israelites, 'The LORD, the God of your fathers—the God of Abraham, the God of Isaac and the God of Jacob—has sent me to you.'
>
> "This is my name forever, the name you shall call me from generation to generation" (Exodus 3:14-15 NIV).

When God says, "I AM WHO I AM," that's the same thing as the name Jehovah. Originally, the name was spelled YHWH, or Yahweh. (It's a little more complicated than that, but this is a good start for now.) When it was translated into

English, it became the name Jehovah. So when you hear the name Jehovah, keep in mind that this is the Hebrew name Yahweh, which means "I am the existing one."

God has so many names, and each one reflects specific things about Him. It's impossible for us to comprehend everything about God—He's just too big and amazing and beyond our imagination—but we can learn more about Him through the names He has revealed to us. And Jehovah is an important one.

What's Your Name?

At the beginning of this book, I asked what happens when someone asks, "What's your name?" You respond with your first name, right? Well, you can think of Jehovah as God's personal name. It's the name God gave when Moses asked, "What's Your name?"

The first name of God we learned, Elohim, refers to God as the one who created the heavens and the earth. The name Jehovah reminds us that God relates to His creation personally. We admire Elohim's creation from afar—look at that colorful sunset! The vast ocean! A breathtaking snowstorm! When God refers to Himself as Jehovah, He's inviting us to get to know Him, just as we would get to know a friend and become closer to him or her as we went through stuff together.

One of the main things we learn about God through His name Jehovah is that He is personal. He is the I Am. God isn't just an idea or an influence or a feeling. He is a living and very personal God who has emotions, intellect, and will. He feels, He thinks, and He makes things happen. He hears us and speaks to us. He is Someone we can get to know.

Think about your best friend. What are your favorite characteristics about him or her?

Look again at the list you just made. Do you see some things that would also be true of God? Maybe you wrote down words like "encouraging" or "likes me no matter what." Those things definitely apply to God! Isn't it amazing that the Creator of the universe can have some of the same characteristics as your best friend? This means you can relate to God personally as you would relate to your friend. How cool is that?

More Than a Friend

We need people in our lives, don't we? It would be really sad to be all alone—to have nobody to eat lunch with, nobody to play with, nobody to fix your dinner, nobody to say goodnight to. But part of God's nature is that He is independent. He needs only Himself to exist in the place where He lives. And He is everlasting.

It's hard for us to imagine this because we're just not that way. That's not how God created us to be. We were created to need friendships and families, and we were also created to need God. But God is totally, 100 percent complete in Himself. When God formally introduced Himself to His people, He basically told Moses, "Tell them that the one who sent you doesn't have to go outside of Himself to be Himself, for He is complete in Himself. I Am who I Am."

This means that God is more than just our friend. We're made in His image, but He is different from us. For one thing, we change. What were you like five years ago? What abilities did you have? What did you like to do? What did you look like? What would someone have said about you back then?

____

____

____

Are you still the same today? Of course not! You've changed. We all change. But God—Jehovah—never, ever changes. He is who He is today, He is who He was yesterday, and He is also who He will be tomorrow because the great I Am never steps out of the present tense. In other words, He is always *now*.

I get that this is really hard to understand! Our minds can understand only what it means to go from one year to the next and then to the next. We turn one age, and then the next year we turn one year older. We enter one grade, and then the next year we enter one grade higher. We grow one inch, and then we grow one inch more. That's how life goes for us. We go from here to there, yet God can go from here to there and back again all at the same time.

Jehovah is our personal God. We can definitely consider Him our friend, but never forget He's way, way more than that. He's the never-changing, always-amazing God of the universe.

Side by Side

Life doesn't always go the way we want it to, does it? Sometimes we have to move and change schools and make new friends. Sometimes parents get divorced. Sometimes family members get sick. Sometimes the world just seems like a really scary place. At times like these, we can grab onto the comfort of knowing Jehovah—the God who never changes and is always there for us.

You'll understand this a little more as you get older, but it's often when a situation is really confusing or crazy that we learn more about God and get to know Him better. Remember Moses? He could have tried to ignore that burning bush and turn the other way, but he got curious. He decided to investigate, and he got to know God and His will in a way that no one ever had.

When God wants to show you a side of Him you've never seen before, He usually does it in the middle of a mess, a problem, a really hard thing...a burning bush. When God tries to get our attention, we need to take notice! He wants to interact with us, to get to know us, and to walk side by side with us through life.

GOD IS WITH US!

Just as we saw Jehovah interacting with Moses in Exodus 3, we see Him interacting with mankind and His creation in Genesis 2. The Lord (Jehovah) God...

"formed man" (verse 7)

"planted a garden" (verse 8)

"caused to grow" (verse 9)

"took the man and put him into the garden" (verse 15)

"commanded the man" (verse 16)

"formed every beast...and brought them to the man" (verse 19)

"caused a deep sleep to fall upon the man" (verse 21)

"took one of his ribs and closed up the flesh" (verse 21)

"fashioned into a woman the rib He had taken" (verse 22)

Jehovah God is right there with us, caring about us, guiding us, and helping us every step of the way.

Get to Know Him

Now you know that Jehovah—the personal God—wants to get to know you. But how do you get to know Him? God is always with us, waiting for us to talk to Him or to read about Him in the Bible or to talk to others about Him, but sometimes we're too distracted to do those things. We might be spending our time on electronic devices or watching TV or listening to music. We get so busy, and our world becomes so noisy, we don't notice what God is saying to us.

But God really, really wants to reveal His plan and His purpose for your life to you. He wants you to experience all the awesome things He has in store for you. And that's why you need to get to know Him—as Jehovah, the Lord. He wants you to get to know Him by the name He used to introduce Himself to Moses and the Israelites in Egypt. Once you get to know God, He will become the main focus of your life. And what an awesome life that will be!

REMEMBER IT!

This might seem a little silly, but sometimes it's the silly things that help us remember. "Jehovah" kind of rhymes with "know ya," doesn't it? And Jehovah is the personal, relational name for God—the name God used when He introduced Himself to Moses. He probably didn't say this (okay, He *definitely* didn't say this!), but imagine God shaking hands with Moses and saying, "Hi, Moses. I'm Jehovah—nice to know ya!" Super corny, I know, but it's easy to remember.

Can you think of any other ways to remember Jehovah, the personal and relational name God uses to remind us He wants to walk hand in hand with us through life? Write them down here.

____

____

____

Jehovah Jireh

The Lord Our Provider

Think of all the kids in your class or in your Sunday school group or on your sports team. You know their first names, right? Of course! But how many of their middle names do you know? The better you know someone, the better your chances of knowing their middle name. The same is true with God. As you get to know Him better, you'll learn more of His names—and you'll understand what they tell you about Him.

In the last chapter, you learned more about God's name Jehovah. When God reveals Himself to someone, He often combines the name Jehovah with another name that reveals something else about Him. In this book, we're looking at the top ten names for God that are important for kids to know. Of those ten names, seven combine the name Jehovah with another name. (They aren't God's first name and middle name, but it might help to think of them that way.)

The name Jehovah Jireh means "the Lord will provide." When someone provides something for you, they give you something useful. Think of your relationship with your parents. They provide a lot of things for you, like food to eat, a house to live in, and clothes to wear. What other things do your parents provide for you? (Hint: Not all of it is material stuff. A hug is something awesome they can provide!)

____

____

____

Trials

You've probably heard of the Olympic Trials. In the Trials, athletes—swimmers, runners, gymnasts, and so on—prove that they are good enough to make the Olympic team. Each sport has different qualifications for making the Olympic team, but all athletes who make it all the way to the Olympics need to go through a selection process first. And they don't just casually show up ready to sprint or jump or throw or dive or flip. No way! These athletes have been through tons and tons of training—conditioning, practicing, monitoring their food, pushing themselves to the limit. There's nothing easy about the Trials!

We can have trials in our own lives too. Our own trials are challenging circumstances that we have to somehow get through. Big things are trials—like losing a family member or having a parent not able to find a job or experiencing a major injury or illness. But smaller things can be trials too—a fight with your best friend, a bad grade on a test, or even exhaustion from not getting enough sleep. Trials are a part of life. They just happen.

Trials aren't fun. No way! But here's something super comforting to remember—every trial must first pass through God's hands before it reaches us. Nothing comes our way without Him knowing about it, and if He knows about it, He must have a special purpose for it. So when something is going wrong, the best thing we can do is to ask, "God, what do You want me to learn from this? What is Your plan here?"

Sports competitions have officials or judges or referees or umpires, right? Think of a few sports—either ones you play or ones you've watched someone else play—and write down what the judges do to make sure the competition is fair.

____

____

____

I love football, so I'm going to use that for my example. In professional football, when a head coach thinks the referee has made a wrong call, he throws out a red flag. This signals that the referee needs to review the play. Sometimes in life, we're tempted to think of God as a referee, and we want to throw out a red flag on Him. "Hey, God, that's not fair!" we might shout. "You need to stop the game. I think You made a wrong call. That wasn't supposed to happen to me!"

But God always knows what He's doing. He doesn't miss anything. He already knows how the game is going to turn out. That's something you can remember when you feel like your life is out of control or no one knows what you're going through. God knows. You can trust Him even in those times. He is often the nearest when He seems the farthest away.

His Perfect Plan

Little did I know growing up in urban Baltimore that I would have a life-changing experience on a neighborhood football field located just a few blocks from my home. And it was a major trial that God used to change the direction of my life.

God works in unusual ways. One day as I ran toward the end zone with the football, a simple cross body block snapped my leg in two. (I still have the steel plate in my right leg from the surgery.) I already had a strong relationship with God, so in that moment, even though I was lying on the football field in horrible pain waiting for the ambulance, I knew that God was in control. I was confident that His will and His ways are perfect even when He asks us to give up the thing we love the most—which for me was football.

I said, "God, You know I love football more than anything. But I'm going to thank You in the middle of this pain and loss. I know You have a plan for my life, and I give You my life to fulfill Your plan." Not long after that, I got involved in full-time ministry, and there's been no turning back. God had a plan for my life, and He used a trial—my broken leg—to get me to that next step in His plan. I trusted that He was going to make sure something amazing came out of the bad situation, which He definitely did!

Regardless of how hard a trial is—like giving up the thing you love the most—you can always know that God has an incredible plan for your life and that every trial has a special purpose. Because of that, we can thank Him in the middle of anything that's going on—a bullying situation, a nasty flu, a move across the country—because we know He can get us through any situation and bring good out of it.

Everyone watching the football game that day saw a leg break. Yet for me, the trial showed me the meaning of the name Jehovah Jireh. God provided a purpose and a direction in my life right in the middle of a very painful trial.

Think about something that is stressing you out right now—something you're spending a lot of time worrying about. Write it down here.

Now, remember that God—Jehovah Jireh—is your provider. He will bring you through whatever you're worried about, and He will give you direction as He shows you more of your purpose in life. What's super cool about this is that not only do you get to know God better, you also get to know yourself better. And you and God get closer. Win-win!

He Gives

Have you ever asked someone, "How many days until Christmas?" I'm sure you have! (In fact, you might even know the answer to that question right now.) For millions of people,

Christmas Day is the best day of the year. The celebration, the gifts, the food...what could be better? Christmas is celebrated in many cultures around the world, each one adding its own ethnic traditions, foods, and music. What are some of the Christmas traditions your family enjoys?

____

____

____

As much as we love the presents and the Christmas carols and the decorations and the cookies, we should always remember that the heart of Christmas is Jesus coming to earth as God's ultimate gift—our Redeemer and Savior. We have the opportunity to have a relationship with a perfect, loving Father who calls us His children. James 1:17 reminds us, "Every good thing given and every perfect gift is from above, coming down from the Father of lights."

But we need to remember something about God—a characteristic He shares with every one of our parents. He doesn't want us to love Him only for His gifts. Imagine how your parents would feel if you told them, "Hey, the only reason I want to live with you and hang out with you is that you give me a bunch of stuff on Christmas. That's the only reason I stick around." They would be heartbroken!

Same with God. He loves us, and because of that He gives us good gifts. But He wants us to love Him apart from His gifts. God is not like a genie or fairy godmother—somebody in a movie or a storybook who exists to grant your every wish. No, God loves giving from His hand as long as He knows that what we really want is to be close to Him. He loves to hear us say, "God, please give me the things that help me to be more like You," or "Please give me gifts that will help me spread Your good news and share Your message with others." He is more than happy to give us those gifts.

He Knows

Have you ever wished you knew everything? That would sure come in handy when taking a math test or reciting Bible verses or working on a science project. But that's never going to happen. Sorry!

The good news is that God knows everything there is to know. He knows what was, what is, and what will be. Nobody can ask God a super hard question that He doesn't know the answer to. God knows everything! The interesting thing about this is that God hasn't necessarily experienced all that He knows. For example, if I were to say, "God, tell me what it feels like to commit a sin," He couldn't answer that question because He's never done it. He's never sinned. Yet because He is the all-knowing God, He understands everything.

Still, even though God has never sinned, He isn't far away from us, knowing and understanding stuff all by Himself. He is a God of experience. And that's part of why He sent His Son, Jesus, to earth. Yes, Jesus came to die for our sins and give us eternal life, but He also came to earth to be a part of the human experience. Hebrews 4:15 says, "We do not have a high priest who cannot sympathize with our weaknesses, but One who has been tempted in all things as we are, yet without sin." Jesus can sympathize with us because He has gone through everything a person can go through except sin.

God really knows us! And because He knows us so well—what we feel, what we need, what we experience—He is able to provide for us.

He Sees

The root word for the name Jireh means "to see." When the names Jehovah and Jireh are put together, they mean "the Lord will provide." The combination of these two names—Jehovah and Jireh—show a relationship between God seeing and God providing.

Let's look at another form of the word "provide." When you hear the word "provision," what comes to mind?

____

____

You might think of "provisions" for a camping trip—things like food and a first aid kit and firewood. But this is a little different. Do you see another word in "provision"? (Hint: Look at the last part of the word.) Write it down here.

____

____

Yep, the word "vision" is a part of "provision." If you have good vision, it means that you can see well, right? So "provision," in this case, means that something was seen ahead of time and was provided for before we even knew we needed it. Because God knows everything, He already knows what we're going to need before we even realize it.

You'll really get to know God as Jehovah Jireh—your amazing provider—as your faith in Him grows. Faith that no matter what you're dealing with—family problems, school issues, friendship troubles, physical challenges, self-confidence struggles—God will get you through it. Your job is to tune in to God, listen to Him, and do what He has instructed you to do—even if it doesn't make sense—simply because He always has your best interest at heart. When you do this, you will see Him provide for you in incredible ways.

And here's one more reminder. Loving God means acting on what He says. It's not just singing songs, praying prayers, or hearing Sunday school lessons or sermons. Many people don't know God as Jehovah Jireh yet. God is waiting for them to act on what He says even though they may not understand how it's going to work out. So keep reading your Bible and listening for His voice and talking to others about Him—He'll let you know what He wants you to do.

You can even keep a journal or a simple list of all the ways God has provided for you. It might be hard to think of things at first, but once you start writing down all the things God has given you and taught you, you'll realize more and more how much He loves you and how many amazing things He has planned and provided for you.

God longs to be Jehovah Jireh to you today. He also wants to see that you're willing to obey Him, to seek Him, and to place Him above everything else in your life. When He watches you honoring Him in this way, you will discover the power of Jehovah Jireh, God the provider, in your life. And you'll realize that He is your source for everything you need. He's got it covered—all of it!

REMEMBER IT!

In order for someone to provide for you, they first need to see what you need, right? And what body part do you need to see something? Your eyes! The first vowel in the word Jireh is "i," which of course rhymes with "eye." Use the space below to draw a picture of an eye and write "Jehovah Jireh provides for me."

Can you think of any other ways to remember Jehovah Jireh, a name for God our provider, who already knows what we need—and Has provided it—before we even realize it? Write them down here.

____

____

____

____

Jehovah Shalom

The Lord Is Peace

We're going to get real here. The world can be a scary place. Even if you don't watch the news, you know that life isn't always peaceful. Schools have lockdown drills. People get mad at each other and fight. Not everything around you is perfectly safe. And sometimes when you think about those things, you can start to feel worried.

But this isn't a chapter about being scared—it's a chapter about having hope. Because we're going to focus on one of the names of God that can give us peace—Jehovah Shalom.

When you hear about bad stuff happening in the news or in your hometown, you can feel as if turmoil rules. Things just aren't very peaceful. And news flash—they never really have been. The world has always had problems. People have always argued with each other. Things haven't ever been rainbows-and-unicorns perfect.

A lot of people today use the word "drama" for turmoil. Life just has drama, doesn't it? Our lives are full of drama—our own or other people's. Even if we try to avoid drama, it's hard to stay away from it. Think back on your week. What kind of drama did you deal with or observe? It could be an argument with your parents, some over-the-top competitiveness (you know, "me first!") at ballet class, or even something you saw on the news. Write down whatever comes to mind.

____

____

This name of God—Jehovah Shalom—speaks directly to our need for calm, security, and stability. It means "the Lord is peace."

Ancient Drama

You might think of drama as something happening today in your life, like a fight between friends or an argument with your brother—which it totally is. But did you know that drama was happening way back in the Old Testament with the Israelites? There was a ton of it!

The Israelites experienced plenty of drama when they escaped from Egypt. Even when they arrived in the Promised Land, things weren't perfect. They still had drama—and kept having it. That's because of a pattern they experienced. The Israelites would start out following God, but then they would stray away from Him and disobey His commands (which were intended to keep things peaceful and drama-free). And that would disrupt the peace and usher in drama. Then they would repent and obey God (which sometimes took a *looong* time!). He would send a deliverer, and the people would experience peace again—until they slipped and the cycle of disobedience started up once more.

You'd think they would have learned their lesson. After all, God got them to the Promised Land. But no! You can still have drama in the Promised Land—I promise.

When we read the Bible, we notice that the Israelites always seemed to rebel and disobey—until they hit rock bottom. Then, with nowhere left to go but up, they remembered, "Oh, yeah. We're supposed to be listening to God! He told us that if we obeyed Him and did what He said, things would go well for us."

Now it's time to be honest. To get real. Has your mom or dad or teacher ever told you, "You need to do what I say or there are going to be consequences." And what happens when you ignore their advice and don't do what they say? Yep—consequences. Things don't go so well. At that point, we come back to them asking, "Why did this happen to me?"

It's the same way with God. Often, people finally cry out to Him when they're dealing with serious drama. And that's when He gently but firmly reminds them that He is the one who saves, protects, and takes care of them.

Back to the Israelites (because they're such a classic example of this). One of their favorite ways to disobey was to turn away from God and adopt other cultures' foreign gods. The Old Testament refers to this as "idolatry." The New Testament calls it "worldliness." But it's the same thing. It's putting your trust in the things of the world and focusing on those things instead of putting God first in your life.

Right now, make a list of things that are important to you or to your friends and classmates. They can be actual things, like electronic devices, or things that aren't material, like popularity. Write them down here.

____

____

____

All of these things on the list are possible idols—things that could come before God in a kid's life. An idol is something you count on for your provision, direction, and satisfaction. It's something that you think will make you happy. It's something you really, really want and spend a ton of time thinking about. And it's something that can get in the way of your relationship with God. When that happens, you're not as connected to God. And you're more likely to worry about stuff and not have peace.

You've Got Talent!

Have you ever had someone see a special talent or skill in you before you did? Maybe it was a parent, a teacher, a coach, or even a friend. (If you're having trouble thinking of something, go ask someone right now. They will let you know.) Write down a few special abilities people have noticed in you.

____

____

____

Sometimes it takes someone else to see a talent, skill, or ability in you that you didn't even know you had. It's really cool when that happens because then you feel confident, and you want to live up to that person's expectation. And their observation might make a big difference in your life.

If your friend says, "You have a great singing voice!" you might decide to join a choir. If your teacher says, "Wow! You're so good with numbers!" you might end up studying math in college and having a job where you work with numbers. If your dad says, "You are so fast!" you might try out for the soccer team or become a sprinter on the track team. This kind of thing happens all the time. You rise to a higher level simply because someone believes in you.

This very thing happened to a guy in the Bible. The angel of the Lord appeared to a man named Gideon. He told Gideon that the Lord was with him, and he addressed Gideon as a valiant warrior (Judges 6:12). But what was Gideon actually doing when the angel told him this? He was hiding—just trying to avoid the drama of the day and survive. Gideon might have thought the angel was making fun of him, but God really did believe in Gideon and sent the angel to let him know.

Gideon's response to the angel and to God was pretty predictable: "Wait—what? Why me? If You are with us, why are things not going so well right now?"

But God had chosen Gideon to get the Israelites back on track and lead them in battle against the Midianites. Of course, He could have chosen anyone or even delivered the Israelites through no person at all. But in this particular case, God chose to throw all His eggs in one basket. "The LORD looked at him and said, 'Go in this your strength and deliver Israel from the hand of the Midianites. Have I not sent you?'"

But then Gideon comes back with this: "O Lord, how shall I deliver Israel? Behold, my family is the least in Manasseh, and I am the youngest in my father's house." Basically, Gideon was letting God know that he wasn't "all that." He didn't think he was anything special. He thought of himself as a nobody.

But maybe that's why God chose Gideon. God often calls ordinary people to do extraordinary things. And it might be for this reason—ordinary people know that they can't accomplish great things all by themselves. They know that they need help and that God can give them the help they need. After all, what do you do when you have to do something that's way too hard for you to do alone? You ask for help. And the harder the job, the quicker you are to say, "Hey, can I have some help here?"

Along with that help comes a sense of peace. God said to Gideon, "Peace to you, do not fear." When Gideon felt God's presence, he knew God as Jehovah Shalom—"the Lord is peace." He found peace knowing God was near.

What Peace Is

If someone were to ask you, "What is peace?" what would you say?

____

____

____

____

A lot of people would respond to that question by saying what peace is *not*. Peace is not fighting with your sister. Peace is not getting mad at your mom. Peace is not going to war with other countries. But there's more to it than that.

Sometimes you and your sister might not be arguing out loud, but you are ignoring each other. It doesn't exactly look or sound like you're fighting, but you're definitely not at peace if you're refusing to acknowledge that the other person exists.

Peace is even bigger than a calm feeling or atmosphere. The word "shalom" means "wholeness, completeness, wellbeing." It means there's no drama happening. It means more than just "it's all good" and more than happiness.

Happiness depends on what happens. For example, your dad could say, "I have an awesome present for you! I'm bringing it home after work." That makes you happy, right? But if your dad gets home from work and says, "Oh, I decided not to bring you a present after all," well, there goes your happiness!

When you have peace, you feel calm inside no matter what's going on around you.

A PICTURE OF PEACE

One day two artists were given the assignment of painting a picture of peace. The one who painted the best picture would win $250,000. As you can imagine, both painters wanted to win.

The first painter set to work by creating a serene portrait of a lake with the sun glistening off of it at just the right angle so it sparkled across the top of the water. The artist added a young girl skipping near the lake with a yellow balloon securely fastened to her wrist. Trees towered gracefully on one side of the lake with birds gathering in their tallest branches.

The second artist had a very different idea in mind when he painted his image. In his painting the sky was pitch black. Lightning zigzagged across the air in unpredictable movements. The painter also had water, but the waves in his painting roared as if they were somehow awakened from a terrible dream. The painting looked more like a portrait of disaster. But way down at the bottom of this scary scene, a little bird stood on a rock. It had its mouth open, singing a beautiful song. One faint light shone down on the bird as it sang.

The second painter won the competition. The judges chose him as the winner because he truly showed what peace is—a feeling of rest and comfort even when everything around you seems frightening.

Being at peace doesn't mean being calm when everything around you is calm. When all is calm, you're supposed to be calm. When the sun is shining and the sky is bright blue and there's no wind, you're not supposed to be freaking out about a terrible storm.

Instead, being at peace means you're at rest even when

everything else seems to be all wrong. It's having faith that God is going to be with you. Jesus said, "These things I have spoken to you, so that in Me you may have peace. In the world you have tribulation, but take courage; I have overcome the world" (John 16:33).

We usually can't control what's happening around us, but we *can* control how we respond to it. We can have peace even when we have problems. If you're home alone in a thunderstorm, you could stand at the window freaking out and imagining all the things that could go wrong. Or you could ask God to give you peace and then turn up some music, get out a coloring book and your favorite markers, play with your dog...whatever it takes to bring peace to your heart and distract you from the storm.

Finding Peace

Some things take a lot of practice. Getting a volleyball serve over the net. Memorizing math facts. Riding a skateboard. You can't just expect to do or know these things right away. Finding peace is the same way. It takes practice—lots of it! You need to spend time hanging out with God and learning about Him and getting to know Him. God promises to give peace to those who keep their minds focused on Him (Isaiah 26:3).

Once you get used to hanging out with God, you'll be more and more inspired to seek Him, His Word, and His ways—and all of these things will help you rest in His peace. When you're scared and worried or dealing with way too much drama, remember God's name Jehovah Shalom. With Him you can always have peace, no matter what's happening all around you.

REMEMBER IT!

Where is your favorite place to be when you're scared or worried or dealing with way too much drama? For a lot of us that place is home. And the word "shalom" rhymes with "home." You can also think of heaven being God's home, and that's where perfect peace comes from. Either way, God's name Jehovah Shalom rhymes with home—and home is where you find peace and rest.

Can you think of any other ways to remember Jehovah Shalom, the name God uses to remind us that He is our peace? Write them down here.

____

____

____

____

Jehovah Rohi

The Lord My Shepherd

You've probably heard stories in Sunday school or church about the Good Shepherd. Basically, it's like this: The Lord is our shepherd, and we are His sheep. Kind of like a parent and child. Well...kind of. Do you know much about sheep? We'll get to that in a minute.

King David wrote the Twenty-Third Psalm, which is that well-known one that begins, "The LORD is my shepherd..." In the name of God we're learning about in this chapter, Jehovah Rohi, Jehovah means "the self-revealing one" and Rohi means "to tend, pasture, shepherd." David was familiar with sheep and shepherding because as a young man, he had been put in charge of his father's sheep. And he saw a bunch of similarities between how he took care of his sheep and how God takes care of us.

If you live in an urban or suburban area like I do, you probably don't often see sheep. And you probably haven't done any shepherding. But everyone knows a shepherd's job is to take care of the sheep.

Just for fun, what do you think a shepherd does? Write down your ideas here.

____

____

____

Kids can expect their parents, grandparents, teachers, and other responsible adults to take care of them. But sometimes we forget that the main one who takes care of us is God. Some people think money will take care of them. Or that they'll be okay if they have a big group of friends. Or talent or success. But God is our shepherd—the one who truly takes care of us.

Look at a couple of things in this sentence: "The Lord is my shepherd." What verb is used?

____

And what tense is that verb written in—past, present, or future?

____

David writes the verb "is" in present tense, meaning that God is taking care of him right now. And he also refers to the Lord as "my" shepherd. This tells us that God is his personal shepherd. So we can learn that the Lord is a personal shepherd—someone we can know and connect with—and a right-now God. This isn't just a Bible story from long ago. It totally applies to life today!

All About Sheep

Okay, right now write down everything you know about sheep—anything at all!

____

____

____

The first thing to know about sheep is that they're dumb. Really dumb. This might sound mean, but it's true. And we're compared to sheep? Ugh! Not good! If a sheep starts walking around in a circle, another sheep will begin to follow it, and then another until the whole flock is walking in a circle...all the while thinking they're going somewhere. It might not be very nice to call something dumb, but sheep just aren't that smart.

Sheep also don't have what it takes to be trained. You've heard of lion tamers and dolphin trainers and dog trainers...but a sheep trainer? No way! Sheep are beyond help when it comes to training.

They're also defenseless. Sheep are easy prey for predators. When a wolf, coyote, hyena, or other hunter approaches a sheep, the sheep has already lost because it has no ability to fight back.

And these poor sheep are also dirty. They can't clean themselves, which is really too bad because they have a thick coat that collects dirt and debris and holds in sweat. Yuck!

Finally, sheep are totally dependent. They aren't good at thinking for themselves. They have to be led by a shepherd if they're going to get anywhere at all. They're directionally and positionally challenged. Sheep don't know which way to go—or even that they are to go at all.

Okay, now look back at those five paragraphs above and write down five things you learned about sheep.

____

____

____

____

____

Sheep need a lot of help, don't they? And that's why they need a shepherd. If we are honest with ourselves, we'll realize that we need a lot of help too. Fortunately, Jehovah Rohi, the Lord our shepherd, is there for us.

Nap Time

If you've had a little toddler in your home, you've probably observed some nap time behavior. When the toddler is obviously tired and worn out and the parent or someone else says, "Sweetie, it's time for your nap," what's the typical response? Usually the little person tries to stall or argue or even throw a tantrum. The last thing she wants to do is lie down. Little Becca might be rubbing her eyes with the backs of her chubby little hands, but she will resist lying down when you suggest a nap. She has no clue how exhausted she really is. She just isn't old enough to understand that she needs to rest.

Yet when you make Becca lie down, she is likely to fall asleep quickly. You aren't making her lie down to be mean to her. You're making her rest because that's what she needs more than anything.

Sometimes God gives us nap time. He does this when we're totally tired and worn out and just not feeling good. When we're exhausted, He also gives us a great place to nap. He chooses the greenest of pastures for our rest. He gives us the softest of mattresses and the fluffiest of pillows because He longs to see us rest and recover, just as we long to see that crying and screaming, worn-out toddler rest and recover.

Like the little toddler, we want to keep doing our own thing and stay awake even though we've completely lost it. But once we rest in God, He restores our sense of hope, purpose, and life. For a toddler, it looks like nap time in her bed. For us, it might look a little different (unless you really and truly need a nap!). You might be super tired from a long week of school and just need to hang out and play games with your family. Or you're worn out from fighting with your sister, and you need to take some time to pray and tell God about your sibling struggles. Maybe your friends are making some bad choices—like making fun of other kids—and you need a break from them. God will help you take that break. God gives you nap time when you need it.

DON'T BE AFRAID

Do you remember taking swimming lessons? Learning to swim can be hard—and kind of scary. But the most important thing in learning to swim is not being afraid of the water. I used to be a lifeguard and water safety instructor. I taught people how to swim. Often the people who sign up for swimming lessons are afraid of water. They want to overcome their anxiety about being in water. So I had a process for teaching them that began with me splashing water on them. I wanted them to get used to the unpredictable nature of water and discover that they could remain safe in it.

The next step was to help them put their heads underwater. Once that was accomplished, I asked them to float on their backs. This was the big test. Lying flat on the water without their feet on the ground was a scary situation for many of them. With nothing beneath them, they felt totally out of control—especially since they didn't know yet how to swim.

But I would place my arms in the water beneath them and assure them that I had them. My arms held them up, and I told them as they lay there that they were safe. Step by step, they learned to feel comfortable where they had previously felt fearful.

Sometimes we don't want to rest and relax

in God's arms. We want to keep doing our own thing, even if we're feeling scared and afraid. But when we understand that God will never let go of us, we can relax and let Him hold us up.

Your Personal GPS

Have you been in the car with your parents when they had their phone direct them someplace? That's how a lot of people get from place to place these days. The voice on the phone tells you where to go—and it can even tell you to go a faster way if there are delays. It's a pretty great system!

In Psalm 23, David writes this about Jehovah Rohi: "He guides me in the paths of righteousness for His name's sake." God guides us, much like a GPS does. (Except God does an even better job!)

Remember the sheep? They need a shepherd to guide them because sheep are prone to wander. And they have no sense of direction! Left on their own, they will regularly take wrong turns. And then other sheep will follow them...and then everyone's all mixed up. That's why sheep need a shepherd. And that's why we need God to give us directions. God, your shepherd, wants to lead you on the right path in each and every decision you make, and He's willing to do that if you seek Him and follow Him. Not only that, but God can also get you back on the right path if you've wandered away.

One day I was in the car with my son Anthony and hadn't turned on the car's navigational system. I'm not that into computers, so I left it off. But Anthony loves anything computerized, so he turned it on. At first, I was a little irritated that he did, so I decided to just follow my own directions and not pay attention to the car's GPS. Unfortunately, I soon realized I was lost. In trying to figure out my own way, I'd gotten off the path that would get us to our destination.

But that's when the navigational system did an amazing thing. A digitized voice said, "Recalculating." And then the GPS gave me a brand-new route to my destination.

This same kind of thing can happen with us and God. We sometimes ignore God's directions and go our own way and do our own thing. But then we end up lost. God—Jehovah Rohi—is even more amazing than a GPS. He can recalculate our location in life and lead us on the path that will take us where He wanted us to go in the first place.

Valleys

Shepherds also guide their sheep through valleys. A valley is a low place between mountains. And it can be a scary place, especially when the sun slips behind a mountain on one side of the valley and the hills cast shadows. Valleys can be dangerous places for sheep. Remember, sheep aren't very smart, so they might think the shadows mean that nighttime is approaching, and they might become afraid. Nighttime is when foxes, wolves, and hyenas come out, which is very frightening for sheep. But the shepherd continually guides the sheep to keep going—even though they might be afraid—as the shadows seem to close in.

Remember what's on either side of the valley? A mountain. From the top of the mountains, you can see everything. You feel like you know what's going on and are a lot more in control. The mountains are where you feel on top of the world. On the mountaintop, it's all good. But you can't go from mountaintop to mountaintop without going through a valley. So remember that Jehovah Rohi, the Lord your shepherd, is with you at all times—even in the darkest, scariest valley.

It's All Good

David finishes Psalm 23 with these words: "Surely goodness and lovingkindness will follow me all the days of my life, and I will dwell in the house of the LORD forever" (verse 6). God's goodness and lovingkindness are continually present in order to guide and lead us in the right direction.

When you know the power of the name Jehovah Rohi, you'll discover that God is able to meet all your needs. Remember how we learned that sheep need a lot of help? And that we need a lot of help too? It's nice to know that God is with us on every mountain and in every valley to give us direction and to point us in the way we need to go. He'll even hold our hand and walk us there.

When the Lord is your shepherd, He's got you covered. He's got your back. And He's taking you to a place that's way more awesome than anything you could ever imagine.

So the question is, is the Lord not only your Savior but also your shepherd? Yes, it's important to believe in Him, but it's also important to follow Him. To recognize that you're a dependent sheep and that you need God to guide you. Through the valleys. Up and down the mountains. Over to green pastures where you can be refreshed with a nap. Jehovah Rohi—the Lord your shepherd—is with you every step of the way.

REMEMBER IT!

Have you ever learned something by assigning meaning to every letter in a word to create a silly sentence? We can use this method to remember that Jehovah Rohi is the Lord our shepherd. Jehovah is a name you have down by now. It's Rohi you need to remember. Sheep can get scared a lot. And what do they do when they get scared? They Run Or Hide Inside. Rohi. See? You can even draw a silly picture of a sheep running or hiding inside something (and add a shepherd finding that sheep!).

Can you think of any other ways to remember the name Jehovah Rohi, "the Lord my shepherd"? Write them down here.

___

___

___

___

Jehovah Nissi

The Lord My Banner

At the church where I pastor in Dallas, Texas, we have two enormous banners hanging on the walls of the sanctuary. One of them has the words, "Lord of lords," and the other loudly proclaims, "King of kings." When you look at these banners from any angle, the words glisten brightly as if to offer their own praise to Jesus Christ.

These banners have hung there for as many years as I can remember, and they are our way of highlighting our conviction that Jesus is both Lord and King over all.

Church isn't the only place where banners are hung. People have used banners all throughout history to show their loyalty to a team or a country or a group.

In the Olympic Games, you'll see athletes enthusiastically wave the flags of the nations they represent. Here in

Dallas, at a Cowboys or Mavericks game, spectators often wave banners as they cheer our teams to victory. I've served the Mavericks as chaplain—which is like the team pastor—for more than three decades, and a few years back, they won the NBA title. At the next season's opening game, they proudly raised the victory banner over a sold-out crowd.

Banners bring people together and get them excited about something. It's as if the banner is saying, "Look! We're all part of the same team! We're all in this together! And we're going to be number one!"

Winners and Losers

In sports there are winners and losers, right? It sounds kind of harsh, but that's basically the way it works. You win a game or you lose it. Sure, sometimes teams will tie, or competitors will win silver or bronze medals, but everyone wants to be number one. Everyone wants the gold medal.

Here's the thing though. Not everyone can be number one all the time. Even the greatest runner or swimmer of all time can have an off race. Even the best gymnast or diver in the world can make a mistake. Even the most awesome team in the world can lose a game. Not everything is going to be perfect all the time.

The true test of a supportive crowd is what they do with their banner when their team doesn't win. Do they start complaining and immediately rip the banner down? Or do they stick with their team because they have faith the team can win again?

We can tell when someone's faith is weakening by the way he or she complains. Complaining from time to time is normal, but when you're constantly complaining and never saying anything positive, that means you're losing faith. You don't expect anything good to ever happen again.

This can happen in our walk with God. When things are going wrong—when we're having a bad day at school or we keep getting sick or our best friend moves away—it's easy to wonder why. And sometimes when we wonder why, we try to figure out where God is when we need Him most.

Don't worry—God hasn't gone anywhere! He's always right there, especially when you need Him most. God is always on your side, and for that reason you should always hang His banner and celebrate His victory. It's okay to complain a little bit—like you might complain when your favorite basketball team misses a few shots in a row—but it's important to stay positive and get back to cheering for your team.

Teamwork

Have you ever been part of a team? When we think of a team, we tend to think of sports that we play with other people, like basketball or football or softball. But you can be part of a team in other situations. Track and field athletes or tennis players are part of a team. Ballet dancers and band musicians are part of a team. You can be in a choir or a scouting organization and be part of a team. Kids in a classroom are part of a team too. What kind of teams have you been on? Write them down here.

____

____

____

All these teams have one thing in common: They all have a leader—a coach, a conductor, an instructor...someone who is in charge of leading and guiding and directing the group. Without the leader *and* the team members, there is no team. That's why they need to work together to do their best. A coach needs to coach her players—not only correcting and instructing them but also encouraging them. A choir director needs to push his singers to perform their very best. A teacher needs to explain and guide and, well...teach!

It's the same with us and God. We are part of His team—we're waving His banner—and we follow Him. But we can't sit back and let Him do it all. We have a responsibility too. A basketball coach could coach and coach and coach, but if the players just sat on the bench doing nothing, what would happen? Yep, the team would lose! A choir leader could direct and direct and direct, but if the choir members never opened their mouths, would the audience hear any music? Nope! It takes both the leader and the team members to make it happen, right?

What do you think would happen if only the leader put in the work?

____

____

____

____

What do you think would happen if only the team members made an effort?

As followers of God, we have a responsibility to do all we can when the game gets tough. Yet unless God also supports us and guides us, our efforts won't be enough.

So what can we do to make sure we're doing our part and contributing to the team effort? Let's say you're struggling in school. Praying about your struggle and asking God to help you is awesome. You should definitely do that! And you can read your Bible for words of encouragement and go to Sunday school to get even more encouragement there. But unless you do something about the actual problem—like talking to your teacher and parents, changing your study habits, or getting extra help—the problem isn't going to just go away on its own. Sure, you need to trust that God is going to help you fix the problem. But if you spend no time doing the practical things you need to do to make things better, you give God nothing to work with.

You can't shift your responsibilities to God. But at the same time, you also can't shift God's responsibilities to yourself. For example, you can't say you're trusting God that you'll get an A on your test unless you cooperate by working hard in school and studying for the test. You need to work together with God as part of a team so that you can fly the banner of victory!

The Bible says, "Working together with him..." (2 Corinthians 6:1). Did you catch that key phrase "with him"? You're a team—you and God. He's your leader, your coach, your teacher—but you need to do some of the work too. Part of having faith is doing your share of the work. It takes teamwork to make things happen.

I Need a Rest!

Sometimes you're doing all you can to be part of the team, but you just get tired. You're running and running all over the soccer field—but then your legs and lungs just get worn out and you can't run very fast anymore. You're practicing over and over for your choir concert, but you suddenly start to lose your voice. You're trying to remember everything for your science test and your math test, but your brain seems to totally shut down and nothing makes sense. These things definitely happen, but that doesn't mean you should quit soccer or drop out of the choir or decide not to take the test. It just means you need a rest. It's okay to tell your coach, "Hey, I need a break. Can you please put someone else in the game?" Or go home a little early from choir practice and drink some tea with lemon. Or take a break from studying and go walk your dog. Rest is important.

Sometimes when you're dealing with an exhausting situation—like family or friend problems or feeling insecure and not very confident—you just want a break from everything. It's okay to take some rest, but be careful that you don't give up on everything. For example, you shouldn't stop praying and reading your Bible and trusting God. And you also shouldn't stop talking to other people and asking them for help.

One of the reasons I love the church is that it provides us with a place to find others who will help us. When life makes you tired, someone can come alongside you to lift you up. Or you can come alongside someone else who's ready to give up and give them the strength to keep going. I often call that piggybacking on someone else's faith when you are tired.

LISTENING

A man in our church came to my house one afternoon when I was preaching a series about God's names. He was really overwhelmed by his problems and wiped out. His head was down, and his hands were limp at his side. He was tired.

"May I come visit you?" he asked on the phone that afternoon before he stopped in. I could hear the tiredness in his voice. "Of course," I said. "Come on over." So he did. And we sat there for about an hour as he talked about the problems in his life. I didn't solve the problems for him. I didn't make everything all better. But I did listen to him and remind him of God's victory, His power, and His presence. And as it was time to go, he left smiling, his head held high.

Sometimes we just need someone to listen to us and reconnect us with God. We need to be there for each other, just like good teammates.

How God Is Our Banner

So how exactly is God our banner? After all, you know what a banner is, but it's a little strange to imagine someone being a banner. The name comes from the book of Exodus.

> The LORD said to Moses, "Write this in a book as a memorial and recite it to Joshua, that I will utterly blot out the memory of Amalek from under heaven." Moses built an altar and named it The Lord is My Banner [Jehovah Nissi]" (Exodus 17:14-15).

We imagine holding up a banner like holding up a flag or a piece of cloth or material. But in biblical times, a banner could refer to any number of items. In this case, the banner was Moses's staff. True, most of us today don't have a shepherd's staff. But God has given us a banner to use for our own challenges of life—His name Jehovah Nissi. When we use this name, we are using God's banner. And we are saying, "The Lord is my banner."

Stuff in life can sometimes get pretty confusing—especially as you get older and you get more responsibilities and school gets harder and you have to make more choices. Sometimes we don't know if we're in or out, up or down, coming or going...life can get crazy! When it does, we need a standard outside ourselves that can tell us what is real and what is not. We need something that can help us make good choices. We need a standard that isn't tied to our emotions, thoughts, or desires. That standard is Jesus Christ. He is our banner.

In the book of Numbers, there's an interesting story that foreshadows—or points to—the coming of Christ.

The Israelites had rebelled against God, so God sent poisonous snakes that bit them. Many of the people died. So they began to cry out to God for mercy.

In answer to their cries, God told Moses to put a bronze snake on a stick and hold it up high (like a banner). He told Moses to let the people of Israel know that whoever looked at the snake up on the stick would live. But everyone who tried to fix the problem all by themselves, without God's help, would die. This is because God had lifted up just one banner, and only those who looked to it lived.

Our banner today is Jehovah Nissi. Whoever looks to Jesus, our banner, will live. It doesn't matter how good you are, how much you try, how much money your family has, how hard you study...all your good efforts will result in nothing if you don't look to Christ, our banner, for your eternal victory. If you do everything in your power to win but aren't connected to Jesus, you will lose. It's that simple.

Even if your situation is hard, Jesus can get you through it. He might not change the situation, but he can always help you change your attitude and your outlook so you can have peace and joy and all those good things in the middle of a not-so-great situation. You can stay positive and encouraging and patient even though at first you might feel like quitting.

So before you decide to give up, look up. What do you see? Jesus, your banner, is there. Your victory has already been won. If Jesus is on your side, you already know the outcome of the game—a win for the home team (yours and God's)! So get pumped and head back into the game. This win will be one worth celebrating!

REMEMBER IT!

If you've ever been in a sporting arena or even a high school gym, you've probably seen banners hanging up that advertise the companies that sponsor a team or school. You can see the banners and logos of restaurants, dentists and doctors, or even car companies. One car company, Nissan, sounds kind of like Nissi. No, God doesn't want everyone to drive a Nissan, but it's a good way to remember the name Jehovah Nissi. The Nissan car company wants you to see the Nissan banner and think that you need a Nissan. When you look up and see the banner Jehovah Nissi, it's God's way of reminding you that you need Jesus.

Can you think of any other ways to remember the name Jehovah Nissi, "the Lord my banner"? Write them down here.

___

___

___

___

Jehovah Rapha

The Lord Who Heals

Have you ever been in a group where people shared prayer requests? Maybe in Sunday school or church camp or a Bible club? At the church where I pastor, we list people's names in the bulletin each week who have asked for prayer for physical healing—people who are sick, people who are having surgery, people who are in the hospital. Every week I pray over those names. And those are just the people who need physical healing. I know that there are many more who need other kinds of healing.

If your best friend moves away and you feel sad, you need healing. If you find yourself getting upset a lot and struggle to control your emotions, you need healing. If you are constantly fighting with your siblings and are worn out from all the arguing, you need healing.

The name of God we're going to look at in this chapter focuses specifically on His power to heal. That name is Jehovah Rapha, "the Lord who heals."

A Watery Miracle

God introduces Himself as Jehovah Rapha, the Lord who heals, right after a great miracle. Do you remember anything about Moses, the Israelites, and the Red Sea? Write down what you remember here.

____

____

You can find this miracle in the book of Exodus. The Israelites had left Egypt, but the Egyptians decided to chase them and take them back to Egypt. The Lord led Israel to the Red Sea, so the Israelites were suddenly caught between a rock and a wet place. Pharaoh was on one side, coming to make them slaves to the Egyptians again, and on the other side stood a very wet and wide body of water—the Red Sea. Yikes! Which would you choose?

____

Tough choice, huh? The Israelites didn't want to go back—and they didn't think they could go forward. They were totally stuck. And that's when God performed a major miracle. He parted the sea, dried up the ground, and allowed the Israelites to pass through to the other side. Then when the Egyptians came in after them, God closed the walls of water, and the Egyptian army drowned.

After that, it's no surprise what the Israelites did. They broke out into a praise and worship service following this awesome miracle by God. There's no way anyone but God could have pulled this off! You'd think they would keep celebrating and celebrating. But no...

Just Right

First the Israelites found themselves facing too much water—the gigantic Red Sea. But as soon as God parted the waters and they crossed the sea, they hit dry land—*very* dry land. On their way from Egypt to the Promised Land, they found themselves in an arid wilderness. The Red Sea had been too wet. This wilderness was now too dry. Why couldn't anyplace be just right?

The Israelites were in a desert wilderness with no water. And three days later, when they eventually did find water, it was undrinkable. "They went three days in the wilderness and found no water. When they came to Marah, they could not drink the waters of Marah, for they were bitter; therefore it was named Marah" (Exodus 15:22-23).

First too much water. Then no water at all. And now bitter, undrinkable water. Ugh! The Israelites needed the healing that water would bring because the human body can only go for so long without water. So what did they do? Did they trust God and remember how He had brought them through the Red Sea? Nope, they started complaining again! Verse 24 says, "The people grumbled at Moses, saying, 'What shall we drink?'"

It didn't take long for the Israelites to forget what God had done—and what God can do.

The Israelites' watery situation teaches us something

important to remember when we're facing a problem—God has a purpose for your pain. He had a reason for allowing the Israelites to have their watery problems: "There He made for them a statute and a regulation, and there He tested them" (verse 25). In other words, water wasn't the problem. Water was a test.

Can You Pass the Test?

If you're a student, you know all about tests, right? Tests might not be our favorite things—especially if we get really nervous taking them—but they do have a purpose. Seriously!

Take a minute to recall all the tests you've taken in the past week or two. What were they, and how did you feel when you were taking them?

When I was in school, my teachers tested me only on things I was supposed to know. I don't remember a teacher testing me on subjects they hadn't taught yet. In fact, no good teacher would test a student on material he or she had not yet covered. A test shows that you were paying attention and that you understand the subject.

The lesson God had taught the Israelites three days before Marah was that He was bigger than water. He was more powerful than water. He was greater than water. God could solve their water problem. And three days after God taught the water lesson, He tested the Israelites on it—He gave them a water test. He did this to see if the Israelites had been paying attention to what He'd been teaching them, and He also did it to show them something new about His character—something that would help them grow and strengthen their faith.

STRUGGLE BRINGS STRENGTH

The story is told of a young boy who discovered a cocoon in a backyard tree. He studied the cocoon carefully, looking for some sign of life. At last, several days later, the boy saw what he had been waiting for. Inside the filmy shell, a newly formed butterfly was struggling to get out.

Filled with compassion for the tiny creature, the boy used his pocketknife to enlarge the hole. Exhausted, the butterfly tumbled out and lay there. But the boy didn't realize that the struggle to escape was designed to strengthen the butterfly's muscles and prepare it for flight. With an act of compassion, the boy had unintentionally crippled the butterfly.

I don't tell you this story to make you sad but instead to encourage you. Struggle brings strength. God knows this, and that's why life has tests. When the time of testing is over, you'll be able to spread your wings and fly high.

Obstacles

Have you ever raced through an obstacle course or watched people race through one on TV? What are some obstacles you have seen competitors get through (or around or across or over)?

Sometimes you can go around obstacles, but a lot of the time you just have to power through them. The night before Jesus was crucified, He prayed to His Father, asking Him not to take us out of the world, but to keep us safe *in* the world. The goal, Jesus realized, wasn't to steer around difficulty, but to navigate safely through it. The obstacles we face in life might be totally tough, but we will always have God's help every step of the way.

A lot of people think that if you're a Christian, life is supposed to be super easy. Not true! Imagine a basketball player stumbling to the sidelines and saying, "Well, coach, I would have scored, but every time I went up to make a shot, some guy from the other team had his hand in my face." Any decent coach would answer, "The guy from the other team is *supposed* to have his hand in your face. That's the way the game is played. It's his job to do all he can to make you miss the shot." In basketball and in life, you're always going to have obstacles.

What would happen if you were taking a test and you laid down your pencil halfway through the test? Even if you had answered each question correctly, quitting halfway through limits your score to 50 percent at best—an F at most schools.

Working through our tests from beginning to end is much easier when we understand that God has a purpose for our problems. It's like the butterfly struggling to escape the cocoon. The point of the escape isn't just to get out of the cocoon. The point is also for the struggle to make the butterfly stronger. The process of getting out is just as important as getting out.

God sends tests to see whether you paid attention when He gave you new information. And sometimes He makes those tests pretty challenging! But He's always given you what you need to pass the tests, so if you have a question about the answer, don't be afraid to go to Him for help.

The Trust Test

You can go to Sunday school or church every week, sing worship songs, memorize Bible verses, attend every kids' activity offered by your church...and assume that your heart, faith, and soul are strong. You can even say, "I love You, God. You are so good. I'll follow You, God. I'll do whatever You say."

But God doesn't simply take your word for it. He tests you and me because He wants what is best for us. He tests us because He is getting ready to do something amazing in our lives. He tests us to see if we're truly trusting in Him.

When God is testing us, He's not being mean to us. He's not an evil teacher who loves seeing students worry and freak out whenever they're given a super hard test. (I hope none of your school teachers are like that either!) His tests are for our benefit—they help us trust in Him. And they're open-book tests. We have access to all the hints and tips we need to pass them. God gives us His Word (the Bible),

Himself, and others who can help us learn more about Him. With all of these awesome resources, you're going to ace God's tests!

Sometimes the solutions to God's tests are kind of unexpected and crazy. Remember the bitter water the Israelites were complaining about? Well, God could have led them to a different drinking source. But He did something else. After Moses cried out to God on behalf of the grumbling group, "the LORD showed him a tree; and he threw it into the waters, and the waters became sweet" (Exodus 15:25).

Tossing a tree into polluted water is definitely an unusual way to make the water drinkable, but that's God for you. He can do anything! And He's way more powerful than any situation or problem.

Here's what I think God was trying to teach the Israelites here: "If you will follow My instructions, I will heal your bodies, emotions, and circumstances. But if you choose to walk the way the rest of the world does, you will not be immune from the world's diseases." It's pretty simple. If you trust in God, He will always help you.

God Makes It Better

Imagine it's summertime, it's 100 degrees out, and you're sweaty and sticky and hungry. What do you want to eat?

___

If you wrote down "watermelon," give me a high five! Watermelon is the best on a super hot summer day.

I was raised in Baltimore, Maryland, and without fail on every Saturday in the summer, my dad would bring home a watermelon. I vividly remember him coming through the door time after time with a big, ripe, juicy watermelon, slicing it open, and giving us each a piece.

Now I live in Texas, and I haven't seen many people here in Texas do what we did next in Maryland. When my dad handed us a slice of watermelon, we put salt all over it. For most of us, salt and watermelon don't seem to go together. In fact, if you're not used to it, the combination might seem totally disgusting. But if you've ever eaten a slice of watermelon with salt on it, you know that the salt makes what is already juicy even juicier. It makes what is already sweet even sweeter. It makes what is already tasty even tastier. It doesn't necessarily make sense to put salt on watermelon, but when you try it, you discover just how yummy it is. In fact, you might have to salt every watermelon you eat from then on!

When you're in need of healing—either healing in your body or healing in your heart—God's way of dealing with your bitter situation won't always make sense. Whether it's a broken bone or a broken friendship, you just want God to stick a Band-Aid on it and make it all better.

But remember, God's ways of healing don't always make sense. Just as God instructed Moses to throw a stick into the water, He may instruct you to do something that seems a little crazy—like putting salt on a watermelon. But when you obey Him and listen to Him and follow His instructions and advice, you will discover that He can turn anything into something far better than you could have ever imagined.

Even in the midst of struggles and bitterness and pain, God has a way to sweeten the waters and heal our bodies, souls, and spirits. He can use the pain and the suffering to make us stronger. He is Jehovah Rapha, the God who heals.

REMEMBER IT!

What do you do when you break or sprain or hurt something? You wrap it. You wrap a broken bone in a cast. You wrap a sprained ankle with a fabric bandage. And you wrap a cut with a Band-Aid. Wrapping whatever is hurt protects it and can speed the healing process. The second part of God's name Jehovah Rapha kind of sounds similar to "wrap." There's even a type of natural fiber called raffia that you use to wrap a present, which sounds a lot like Rapha.

Can you think of any other ways to remember the name Jehovah Rapha, "the Lord who heals"? Write them down here.

____

____

____

____

Jehovah Tsidkenu

The Lord Our Righteousness

If you don't like a TV show, what can you do? You can find another show you like (or better yet, turn off the TV!). What happens when you decide baseball is no longer fun? You can try a new team with a new coach—or you can try track or lacrosse or another sport. And if you don't like a subject in school? Well, not so fast there! Sometimes we need to stick with things whether we like them or not.

We can have the same reaction to God and His Word. Sometimes everything is going along fine, but then suddenly we don't like what He tells us to do or He gives us a solution to our problem that we don't agree with. And when that happens, we have two choices. We can either listen to God, ask for His strength, and do what He says (and have a good outcome), or we can plug our ears, turn the other way, and do something totally different (and have a bad outcome).

The Israelites were plugging their ears and turning the other way when God revealed the next name we will learn about. They had stopped following the one true God and were following foreign gods that the Israelites thought were more in tune with what they wanted to do. At this point, they discovered the next name of God—Jehovah Tsidkenu, "the Lord our righteousness." (You pronounce it "sid-kay-new.")

Turning Away

What happens when someone is talking to you and you turn away from them and start walking in the opposite direction? How do you think the conversation would go? Write down your answer here.

____

____

____

____

Not very well, right? You would have no idea what that person was saying to you, and you probably wouldn't end up having a very good conversation. It's the same way with God. When you turn away from Him, you don't get to hear what He is telling you. You miss out on His guidance and direction and instruction. And then you *really* start to have problems.

This happened with the leaders of the Israelites, whom God called their shepherds. (You remember all about shepherds and sheep, don't you?) Jeremiah 23:1 says, "Woe to the shepherds who are destroying and scattering the sheep of My pasture!" God says that the shepherds—those who were leading the people—were creating a lot of confusion by not following God. And because the shepherds weren't following God, the sheep—the rest of the people—weren't following Him either. What a mess!

In fact, rather than using their position of influence to guide and direct God's people toward Him, the leaders were actually driving the people away from God. That's why God had to give them such a stern warning. They had already messed up, and He didn't want them to get any further away from Him.

Choices

Okay, so you're not physically turning away from God and walking the other way. But there's another way to walk with God (or away from Him). You have choices to make every day—choices that are distinctly right or wrong. And if you make a wrong choice, that's like walking away from God. Cheating on a test or not cheating on a test. Making fun of other kids or not making fun of them. Telling a lie or not telling a lie.

What is the first part of the word "righteousness"?

____

And what is the opposite of right?

____

I'm sure your two answers above were "right" and "wrong." God says that when we choose to do what is right, we won't be afraid. We will be saved, and we will have peace. So it sounds like we definitely should do what is right!

Sometimes people will try to tell you that something isn't necessarily right or wrong. A kid in your class might say, "It's okay to cheat on a test because then you get a good grade, and that's what's most important." But that's not true. Being honest is more important than getting a good grade. And maybe you don't do well on the test because you struggled to understand the material. You might have a chance to relearn the material and take the test again. If you cheat, it's eventually going to catch up with you. And the results of that are way worse than a poor grade.

Different people can have different opinions about what is right and what is wrong, but there's one standard you can always count on. God is the benchmark by which everything else should be measured. He is the dividing line that separates right from wrong. His name is the name by which we can be able to tell good from bad.

Righteousness comes from God, so only He can define true righteousness. Wrongness can be understood as anything that goes against God's righteousness.

The Bible gives a special blessing to those who follow God and do what is right. Matthew 5:6 says, "Blessed are those who hunger and thirst for righteousness, for they shall be satisfied."

When you go to the doctor for a checkup, the doctor often asks you about your eating habits. If you aren't very hungry—or if you only eat certain foods—something could be wrong. You could be sick or be allergic to something. It's the same thing with righteousness. When you lose your appetite for it, something is wrong with you spiritually. As you grow in your faith and get to know Jesus better, you will be hungry for righteousness.

Snack Time

If your hunger for doing what is right is decreasing and your hunger for doing the wrong thing is increasing, you can be sure the distance between you and God is growing. This reminds me of a conversation I had with my son Anthony not long ago. He told me he sometimes struggles to maintain his weight because he loves to snack. "The problem is," he said, "when I snack, I don't feel like eating 'real' food. So I fill up without the nutrients."

When you think of the yummiest snacks, what pops into your mind?

____

____

____

And when someone mentions "real" food, what do you think of ?

____

____

If you listed snacks like chips and candy and cookies, and if you included apples and carrots and chicken in the "real" food category, you understand the difference between good and bad food choices. But just because we know the difference doesn't mean we always make the best choices.

You can go to the donut shop and get full. But a donut is nutritionally "wrong." It might be "right" in terms of sweetness and pleasure, but considering what your body needs to function, it's wrong. If you fill up on donuts, you'll lose your appetite for "real" food that supplies you with vitamins, minerals, complex carbohydrates, and all those good things. You'll lose your hunger for what is good for you, and as a result you won't eat as much healthy food.

Choosing unhealthy food is bad for your body. And other unhealthy choices are bad for your heart. When you fill up your heart and mind by watching mindless TV shows, playing computer games for hours, or hanging out with kids who are constantly complaining, those things affect your heart. They make you lose your appetite and hunger for the things of God and the things that are good.

God is righteousness. His viewpoint is the right viewpoint. His directions are the right directions. If you plug your ears and walk away from Him, you will miss all that is good.

Act First, and Feelings Will Follow

Have you ever not felt like doing a chore? What are some of your least favorite chores to do?

___

___

___

Sorry, I'm not going to give you space to make the list longer! You might not feel like folding your clothes and putting them away, but after you do, it's nice to have a closet full of clean clothes to wear. You might not feel like getting up early to let the dog out, but when you do, you're rewarded with a happy pup. You might not feel like doing your homework when the sun is shining outside, but it's great to get it done so you have the rest of the afternoon to play.

As you can see, choosing the right actions can change your feelings. You can go from being grumpy and complaining to being happy and relieved—all because you took action and did the right thing.

Righteousness may not always feel good at first. In fact, it may hurt. But the results of righteousness in your life will be good. Because Jehovah Tsidkenu, "the Lord our righteousness," is one of God's names, He cannot take part in unrighteousness.

We know that doctors and bacteria don't go together in the surgery room. If doctors didn't wash their hands or wear gloves before performing surgery, some major problems would occur. Patients would probably get infections that would prevent them from healing well.

Because God is righteous, one of His jobs is to show you where sin and bad choices have infected your life. And once the sin is out there to deal with, you can ask God for forgiveness, deal with the problem, and return to a right relationship with God.

So choose your actions wisely. Do your best to know the difference between right and wrong, and if you're confused, talk to God about it. The more you read your Bible, the better choices you'll be able to make. You can also ask more mature Christians—like your parents, older siblings or cousins, or your Sunday school teacher—to help you when you're confused about a decision you need to make. Chances are they have been through a similar situation and will have some great advice for you.

Growing Righteousness

Do you have a garden at home? If you do, write down what plants are growing in your garden. Flowers? Vegetables? Trees? Bushes? (If you don't have a garden, write down what you imagine would be growing in one if you did.)

____

____

____

____

Each of the plants and trees growing in your garden started from a seed. Did you know that God plants seeds inside us? These are seeds of righteousness, and if you want them to grow—just like you want the flowers and vegetables in your garden to grow—you need to take care of them. Plants need water and sunlight, right? If they didn't have those things, they would die. And if we don't feed and nourish the seeds of righteousness inside us, they too will die.

There are several ways you can feed and nourish the seeds of righteousness planted in your spirit. One way is by reading and obeying the Word of God. Another way is to "put on" Christ. The apostle Paul wrote, "Put on the new self, which in the likeness of God has been created in righteousness and holiness of the truth" (Ephesians 4:24). And "put on the Lord Jesus Christ" (Romans 13:14). Okay, that sounds a little funny—"putting on" Christ. Let me explain.

When you get dressed in the morning, what do you put on?

____

____

____

____

Besides your clothes, every day when you wake up and get dressed, you can put on Jesus Christ. And you can continue putting on Jesus Christ as you go throughout your day. You do this by wearing His righteousness—choosing to do what He asks you to do. You look at life and situations through His eyes and make your choices based on the choices He would make.

As you continue to do this day by day, moment by moment, you grow to be more like Jesus. The righteous seed in you grows too. As it grows, it transforms everything about you—your attitude, your actions, your feelings...your entire self. And suddenly you're not forcing yourself to do the right thing and make the right choices. Instead, you're making those good choices automatically.

When you're trying to figure out whether something is right or wrong, the best thing to do is to ask yourself, *What does God think about this?* Keep in mind that you need to ask yourself that question first—before asking your friends. Don't just ask the kid sitting next to you in class or your buddy on the soccer team. If you've talked with God about it but aren't sure what He wants you to do, then ask a more mature Christian. Don't jump in and do something until you're pretty sure you know how God feels about it. Things will go so much better for you if you check with Him first—I promise!

You can't hang around with the wrong friends and expect to have the right life. You can't make bad choices and expect things to go well. You can't plug your ears and walk away from God and expect to automatically know the right thing to do. If you want to grow in righteousness, hang out with people who are also pursuing righteousness. Stick close to God. Talk to Him. Read His Word. Hang out with people who are also following Him. And you'll grow and grow to be more like Him—which is good and righteous and amazing.

REMEMBER IT!

We have come to a super tough name to remember—probably the hardest name in this entire book! Jehovah Tsidkenu, "the Lord our righteousness." First of all, a little reminder on how to pronounce Tsidkenu—it's "sid-kay-new." We're going to focus on that last syllable—"nu," which is pronounced just like our word "new." When we seek God, He makes our lives brand-new. We looked at Ephesians 4:24, which tells us to "put on the new self." When something is new, it is bright and shiny and works perfectly. That's what we want to be—and Jesus makes us brand-new!

Can you think of any other ways to remember God's name Jehovah Tsidkenu, "the Lord our righteousness"? Write them down here.

El Shaddai

Lord God Almighty

One of my favorite names of God is El Shaddai, which means "Lord God Almighty." It's a powerful combination of *El* ("God") and *Shaddai* ("almighty, sufficient"). We're introduced to the name in Genesis 17 when Abraham (who was still called Abram) receives a visit from the Lord.

> When Abram was ninety-nine years old, the LORD appeared to Abram and said to him,
>
> "I am God Almighty" [El Shaddai];
> Walk before Me, and be blameless.
> I will establish My covenant between
> Me and you,
> And I will multiply you exceedingly" (verses 1-2).

God introduces Himself to Abram (and us) as El Shaddai through a covenant, which is a formal, official agreement. Those who trust in Jesus Christ as their personal Lord and Savior have entered into what is called the "new covenant." You might recognize those two words—they're from the Bible, and they're often read during Communion (or the Lord's Supper) at church: "This cup is the new covenant in My blood; do this, as often as you drink it, in remembrance of Me" (1 Corinthians 11:25).

God made His covenant with Abram when Abram was 75 years old. That was when God told Abram He had a special plan for him and a special blessing.

Blessings

Think back on this past year...what are some of the best things other people gave to you or did for you?

____

____

Things people give to you or do for you or even say to you are all *blessings*. You didn't do anything to earn them. Others just give them to you because they think that you're special and that you deserve them.

God gives blessings to all of us. In fact, His covenants always involve blessings. A blessing is something God gives you or does for you or promises you—so that you can share it with others and bring Him glory. A blessing is never only what God does to you. It has to go full circle in order for it to be a blessing. A blessing is what God does to you so that it might flow through you to others.

Think about some of the blessings that other people have given to you and that you can share with even more people. Maybe you learned to knit and received knitting needles and yarn for Christmas. You could knit scarves or socks to give to people who need warm clothes. Or someone gave you a compliment: "You're so patient and so kind." You could take that compliment and run with it—maybe helping with the toddlers at church or helping welcome the new kids at your school. Someone gives you something, and you use that blessing to help others. That's the way God intended for blessings to work.

So when God told Abram He had a special plan and a special blessing for him, it wasn't just a promise to give good things to Abram. Rather, God said He would bring about good to Abram and make him into a great nation so that "all the families of the earth will be blessed." Talk about a blessing that has a major effect!

Promises

Sometimes people give us promises, but they seem to take forever to come. "I haven't gotten your birthday present yet," your friend tells you, "but I promise I'll get it soon!" Or your parents promise you'll go camping someday, but it seems like every weekend is too busy. Even little promises—"I promise I'll get ice cream at the store"—can sometimes not turn out. Your mom or dad forgets the ice cream, and there goes that promise.

Your family and friends don't usually mean to break their promises, but it happens. Life happens. Here's the wonderful thing about God—He never breaks His promises. He never gets too busy. He never forgets. Sure, sometimes it might seem as if He's taking forever to fulfill His promise.

But don't worry—He's got this. If He says He will make something happen, He will make it happen!

Remember, He is the Creator God who can make something out of nothing (Hebrews 11:3) and sustain life all on His own. He is El Shaddai, the Lord God Almighty. He'll work it out. You don't have to figure it out on your own. God's got it. He can do anything! Keeping promises? He can totally do that—every single time.

God does what He says He will do simply because He is faithful to His promises and covenant. He has the power to make anything happen. He can do the impossible—like creating the heavens and the earth out of nothing at all. In fact, He loves to do the impossible for us!

Hanging Out with God

Have you ever felt so tired you didn't really want to do anything? Even if you're someone who's normally full of tons of energy, you can still have those occasional lazy days. When I'm feeling down or low on energy, I love reading Psalm 91. Here are the first two verses:

> He who dwells in the shelter of the Most High will abide in the shadow of the Almighty [Shaddai]. I will say to the LORD, "My refuge and my fortress, My God, in whom I trust!"

Whether you're trying to make things happen yourself or you've given up trying to make things happen, everything will work better if you hang out with God. Just imagine yourself stringing a hammock between two trees, climbing into it, and letting God gently rock you back and forth in the breeze. Nice, huh?

If you hang out where God hangs out—"in the shelter of the Most High"—He'll do His thing in your life. He'll be your El Shaddai. God wants to spend time with you. He wants to build a relationship with you. He wants you to have faith in Him. Right after revealing His name El Shaddai, God told Abraham, "Walk before me" (Genesis 17:1). In the same way, God wants you to hang out with Him and walk before Him all the time.

Jesus puts it this way: "I am the vine, you are the branches; he who abides in Me and I in him, he bears much fruit, for apart from Me you can do nothing" (John 15:5). To abide with someone is to hang out with him. All the time. And Jesus also tells us, "If you abide in Me, and My words abide in you, ask whatever you wish, and it will be done for you" (verse 7). What a promise! And all that's required of you is hanging out with Jesus. That's a pretty sweet deal.

HOW BIG IS YOUR FRYING PAN?

One day a man went fishing with his friend, and before long, he caught a fairly large fish. He quickly took it off the hook and threw it back in the water. A few minutes passed, and he caught another huge fish. Again, he unhooked it and tossed it back in. His friend assumed he was fishing for sport and not for food, but then the man caught a smaller fish and kept it.

"I don't understand," the friend said. "Why are you throwing the big ones back but keeping the small one?"

His friend replied, "My frying pan is only ten inches wide."

Friend, sometimes we're so accustomed to the way we have always done things, we don't realize God wants to do something even bigger in us and through us to bless others. If we settle for what we can do on our own, without God's help, we won't experience the miracles that El Shaddai wants to do in us. Don't be limited by the size of your frying pan, because it will always be too small. Rather, look at the size of your great and amazing God and remember His name—El Shaddai, the Lord God Almighty.

Keep the Faith

What does the word "faith" mean to you? Write down your answer here.

____

____

There are so many great stories of faith in the Bible, but one of the best ones is found in Daniel 3:20. King Nebuchadnezzar "commanded certain valiant warriors who were in his army to tie up Shadrach, Meshach and Abed-nego in order to cast them into the furnace of blazing fire."

These dudes, Shadrach, Meshach, and Abed-nego, were in a bad situation. It doesn't get much worse than being thrown into a furnace—except for being thrown in bound hand and foot. However, these three young men put their faith in God, and something awesome happened.

> Then Nebuchadnezzar the king was astounded and stood up in haste; he said to his high officials, "Was it not three men we cast bound into the midst of the fire?" They replied to the king, "Certainly, O king." He said, "Look! I see four men loosed and walking about in the midst of the fire without harm, and the appearance of the fourth is like a son of the gods" (verses 24-25).

God honored these three young men's faith by delivering them from the danger of the fiery furnace even when they were standing in the middle of it. That's proof that if you hang out with Him and have faith in Him, He can get you through anything.

And Also Have Hope

That's faith—relying on God to get you through even in the scariest situation. Now we're going to talk about the word "hope." What do you think it means? Write down your idea here.

___

___

You can have all the faith in the world, but that doesn't mean life is always going to go perfectly. You can have faith that you'll never get sick or that you'll get 100 percent on every test or that you'll have a perfect score in your gymnastics meet, but are those realistic things to have faith in?

Of course not! You will get sick—even if it's just a cold. You won't get 100 percent on every test—sooner or later you will answer a question wrong. And you won't have a perfect score in every gymnastics meet you compete in—even a tiny mistake on your floor exercise will keep you from getting a perfect score. It's just not realistic to expect perfection in this world.

The Bible is full of good news—the gospel—but that doesn't mean that bad things will never happen. Christians face the same troubles other people do. However, if you're a Christian, you have hope—you can be confident that God always keeps His promises.

God is aware of everything you're going through—from problems with math facts to parents getting a divorce to just a general fear that something bad is going to happen. And He is working to keep His promises to you—to never leave you, to walk beside you, and to bless you. No matter what your situation is and how long you've been asking Him to help you get through it, keep your faith in God because He will always keep you safe and with Him. Even if you can't see any answers to your problems, keep building up your faith in Him.

Remember what the name El Shaddai means? "Lord God Almighty." If someone is almighty, that means they have more power than anyone or anything else. Obviously, only one person can be almighty—and that totally describes God. He has more power than anyone you can imagine—way more than every superhero put together!

So God, the Almighty, has this. He's already won! And when the day comes for your victory, when your difficult situation is resolved in a way that helps others and brings Him glory, praise Him. Praise Him because He saw you through what seemed like a hopeless situation. Getting back to Abraham, Romans 4:18 says, "Against all hope, Abraham in hope believed" (NIV). And God answered his prayer.

You, too, will see the fruit of your belief. It's a promise from God, who says, "Those who hope in me will not be disappointed" (Isaiah 49:23 NIV).

Blessings. Promises. Faith. Hope. We've covered so many good things in this chapter! So learn to recognize God's blessings—and then go and use them to bless others. Read about His promises, listen for them, and rejoice when what He promised you comes true. Have faith that He can accomplish anything, and thank Him for His goodness. And when you're feeling frustrated and you wonder if anything is going to turn out all right for you, have hope—because He's the Lord God Almighty, and He can do anything.

Put your hope in El Shaddai today. He knows you. He loves you. And He will be there for you, walking side by side with you when you trust Him to fulfill His promises in you and through you.

REMEMBER IT!

You pronounce the name El Shaddai like this: "Ell shad-eye." "Shad" sounds a little bit like "shade." And "eye"? Well, it sounds like...eye! Remember how we talked about hanging out in your hammock with God and resting with Him—in the "shadow of the Most High"? If it's a really hot day, where would you hang up your hammock? In the shade, right? Also, "shad" is the first part of shadow. So if you remember "shade" or "shadow" followed by "eye," you should be able to remember El Shaddai.

Can you think of any other ways to remember this name—El Shaddai, Lord God Almighty? Write them down here.

____

____

____

____

Immanuel

God with Us

If you were to come over to my house at Christmastime, you would notice a number of fairly large gift boxes, all wrapped and sitting near the front door of our home. These colorful decorated boxes totally say Christmas. They have all the glitter and shine of the holiday season, and they're tied up with great big bows.

There's only one problem. These boxes are empty. They're not presents at all. If someone were to steal them when we were gone, they would just get decorations. The packages look like Christmas presents, but they have no meaning or value inside.

These packages are kind of like some Christians today. Some people totally dress up for church and carry a Bible under their arm and can quote a whole bunch of verses.

But if we were to peel away the paper and tape and bows, we wouldn't see much of Jesus inside. And without Jesus, Christianity would be nothing special.

Immanuel is the final name of God we're going to learn, and it's connected to all the names we've learned so far. The record of Jesus's birth includes these words:

> "She will give birth to a son, and you are to give him the name Jesus, because he will save his people from their sins."
>
> All this took place to fulfill what the Lord had said through the prophet: "The virgin will conceive and give birth to a son, and they will call him Immanuel" (which means "God with us") (Matthew 1:21-23 NIV).

You might have heard this passage read around Christmastime, and you might recognize the name Immanuel (sometimes written as Emmanuel) from Christmas stories and songs. But it's not just about a baby being born, miraculous as that may be. Isaiah 9:6 says, "For to us a child is born, to us a son is given."

The child is born, but the Son of God is given. That's because the Son existed before the child was born. It might sound a little confusing, but because Jesus is the Son of God, He has always been and always will be.

Jesus came not only to do the Father's will but also to represent God the Father so that we would know what it's like to have God with us. That's what the name Immanuel tells us.

Jesus Christ is Immanuel, God with us. He is the image and likeness of God, sent to show us the beauty and majesty of the King. Jesus Christ didn't just show up for the first time on that first Christmas morning in Bethlehem though. He existed before creation, "in the beginning."

Can you remember some of the things Jesus did while He was living here on earth? Write them down here.

Jesus walked among us. He was completely human, yet He was also completely God. That's one of those concepts that's really hard to understand, but we just need to believe it and accept it and know that it's true. For example, one moment He was hungry because He was fully human, and the next moment He miraculously fed 5000 people because He was God.

What's in a Name

Earlier in this book, we talked about the reasons your parents may have chosen your name for you. Maybe you were named after a relative or friend, or they just liked the way your name sounded. In Bible times, though, parents cared less about how a name sounded and more about its meaning. A name told something about that person.

When the angel Gabriel visited Mary to tell her about the birth of the Messiah, he instructed Mary to call the baby Jesus because that name meant He would save His people from their sins. Jesus is the New Testament equivalent of the Old Testament name Joshua, which means "salvation."

Yet Jesus has other names as well. They aren't literal names you would use when talking to someone. They are descriptive names that let us know a little bit more about who He is. Look at Isaiah 9:6: "He will be called Wonderful Counselor, Mighty God, Everlasting Father, Prince of Peace." Have you ever been called any of these things—or known anyone who has been called these things? Probably not! They're pretty unusual—and most likely a little unfamiliar. So let's briefly take a look at each of them.

Wonderful Counselor

I'm a pastor, so I counsel members of our church. I usually try to do a good job, but the kind of advice people receive depends on the kind of day I'm having. I do my best, but I'm not perfect. I haven't gone through everything and experienced everything, and I definitely don't know everything.

That's what makes Jesus the Wonderful Counselor. His perspective is infinite—He's always existed. His experience includes a lifetime on earth dealing with the same stuff we face. Nobody could ever give us better guidance and direction and advice!

How is Jesus the Wonderful Counselor to you?

___

___

Mighty God

Jesus never fails. He is faithful. All the power of creation stands behind His promise to provide for us and care for us. He is strong and wise and capable of doing absolutely anything at all.

Jesus can turn some crackers and sardines into a lunch for thousands of hungry people simply by believing and offering up a thank-you in faith. He has the power to calm the stormy seas by simply saying the word "peace." The hands that formed the mountains, oceans, and skies are strong enough to defeat any enemy yet gentle enough to comfort any heart. When we say someone is mighty, we're talking about more than just strength. Might is the ability to use your strength for the good of others. Jesus—Immanuel—shows us might in its most perfect form.

How is Jesus the Mighty God to you?

Everlasting Father

Remember when we tried to wrap our brain around the idea of God being infinite and always existing? That was so hard to understand, wasn't it? The good news is that we don't have to understand. We just need to believe.

After you've gone back as far as you can imagine, you're no closer to the beginning of God than when you started. "Everlasting" means forever! There is no beginning. There is no end. The main thing is that God has always been here.

How is God the Everlasting Father to you?

Prince of Peace

People in our world really want peace. World leaders sit around tables and try to come to agreements for peace.

Teachers meet with kids who are arguing and fighting and try to figure out some kind of plan for peace. Parents and children have family meetings to find a way to stop the arguing and have a peaceful home. But usually the peace isn't permanent and the fights and arguments and disagreements start all over again.

Few of us actually understand peace. But in Jesus, we can find peace. That's because He is the Prince of Peace. The apostle Paul discovered this truth, and here's what He said about peace:

> I have learned to be content whatever the circumstances. I know what it is to be in need, and I know what it is to have plenty. I have learned the secret of being content in any and every situation, whether well fed or hungry, whether living in plenty or in want. I do all this through him who gives me strength (Philippians 4:11-13 NIV).

Some people think that peace is the absence of arguing and fighting. But remember how you could ignore your sister and still not be at peace? Jesus, the Prince of Peace, promises us a peace that is beyond our understanding and totally amazing.

How is Jesus the Prince of Peace to you?

____

____

____

____

ONE MORE TIME

Let's briefly recap all the names of God we've learned in this book. We'll also see how the New Testament shows that Jesus, the Son of God, is the "exact representation of His nature" (Hebrews 1:3).

- Elohom (the strong Creator God): "In [Jesus] all things were created: things in heaven and on earth, visible and invisible, whether thrones or powers or rulers or authorities; all things have been created through him and for him" (Colossians 1:16 NIV).

- Jehovah (the relational God): "May [those who believe] be one as we are one—I in them and you in me—so that they may be brought to complete unity. Then the world will know that you sent me and have loved them even as you have loved me" (John 17:22-23 NIV).

- Jehovah Jireh (the Lord our provider): "I am the bread of life. Whoever comes to me will never go hungry, and whoever believes in me will never be thirsty" (John 6:35 NIV).

- Jehovah Shalom (the Lord is peace): "I have told you these things, so that in me you may have peace" (John 16:33 NIV).

- Jehovah Rohi (the Lord my shepherd): "My sheep listen to my voice; I know them, and they follow me" (John 10:27 NIV).
- Jehovah Nissi (the Lord my banner): "In this world you will have trouble. But take heart! I have overcome the world" (John 16:33 NIV).
- Jehovah Rapha (the Lord who heals): "Jesus went throughout Galilee, teaching in their synagogues, proclaiming the good news of the kingdom, and healing every disease and sickness among the people" (Matthew 4:23 NIV).
- Jehovah Tsidkenu (the Lord our righteousness): "God made him who had no sin to be sin for us, so that in him we might become the righteousness of God" (2 Corinthians 5:21 NIV).
- El Shaddai (Lord God Almighty): "'I am the Alpha and the Omega,' says the Lord God, 'who is, and who was, and who is to come, the Almighty'" (Revelation 1:8 NIV).
- Immanuel (God with us): "'She will give birth to a son, and you are to give him the name Jesus, because he will save his people from their sins...And they will call him Immanuel' (which means 'God with us')" (Matthew 1:21-23).

Knowing Jesus

Knowing Jesus personally will totally change your life! But just knowing *about* Him won't do much good. For example, I know about the president. I can tell you his name. I can even tell you his address. I can tell you some information I've heard about him. But that doesn't mean I know him.

What can you do to get to know a friend better?

____

____

In order to truly know Jesus Christ, you need to spend time with him. You need to talk to Him. Hang out with Him. Discover more about Him. And see what He wants to do with, in, and through you.

Jesus has an awesome plan for your life. He has a purpose and a path for you. If you want to get to know your plan and your purpose and your path, get to know the One who knows it best—Jesus. The closer you get to Jesus, the more you understand how to live this amazing thing called life.

Immanuel the Celebrity

We live in a day of celebrities. Famous people are all around us. Who are the first five celebrities that come to your mind? Write down their names here.

____

____

____

____

____

We admire many people because of their ability to act, sing, compete athletically, and so on. However, over time, we lose interest in most celebrities. Their skill, talent, or fame declines, and they are soon forgotten. In fact, try asking your parents or grandparents who some famous people were when they were kids. Chances are, you haven't even heard of some of these individuals!

Yet Jesus Christ—Immanuel—will never lose His status. He never wrote a song, and yet there are more songs written about Him than any other person who has ever lived.

He never wrote a book, and yet the book written about Him has outsold every other book.

He never traveled more than 300 miles from the place of His birth, and yet people on every corner of this earth recognize His name.

Although Jesus is the greatest celebrity ever to live, He didn't spend His days on earth in a Hollywood mansion or traveling the world in a private jet. He could have been born in a castle and appeared to the world as a king, but then so many of us would not have been able to relate to Him. So He came as a baby, born in a barn. And He didn't exactly live the life of the rich and famous—He was born to poor parents in the middle of a world filled with chaos.

The good news of Jesus Christ is that it doesn't matter who you are or where you live or what you look like. It doesn't matter if your family is rich or poor or somewhere in between. It doesn't matter if you are shy or outgoing, athletic or artsy, a boy or a girl, a city kid or a farm kid. He knows you. And He came to this world for you, to bring you salvation by taking on the sins of the entire world and dying on the cross.

Through the name of Jesus, every single person on earth is able to receive the incredible gift of eternal life. By faith in His name and in His death, burial, and resurrection, we are given the gift of salvation. He is Immanuel—God with us—and He is with you, loving you and caring for you and leading you now and forever.

REMEMBER IT!

The trick we're going to use to remember this tenth and final name of God, Immanuel (God with us), has to do with Jesus being born on earth as a baby and living among us. Remember, Jesus was fully God and fully man. The word "man" is in the middle of the name Immanuel. Jesus lived on earth—with us—as a man, walking and talking with people and experiencing all the highs and lows of life.

Can you think of any other ways to remember the name Immanuel, God with us? Write them down here.

Good to Know You!

I hope that as you've traveled on this journey of learning the names of God, you've done more than just memorize the names and their meanings. I hope that you've gotten to know more about God and that you've gotten to know Him more. Because knowing God is the single most important thing you'll ever do in your life. Nothing is more valuable than a personal relationship with Him and living life with Him by your side.

If you're not sure that you really know God, and you would like to accept His love and salvation, please take the time now to talk with your parents or Sunday school teacher or summer camp counselor or another mature Christian. He or she can pray with you and help you begin the awesome experience of being a follower of Jesus Christ.

Right now would be a great time to write down a few things you've learned about each name of God. I'll list the names (and their meanings), and you write down a few things you discovered about each one:

1. **Elohim** (the strong Creator God):

____

____

____

2. **Jehovah** (the relational God):

____

____

____

3. **Jehovah Jireh** (the Lord our provider):

____

____

____

4. **Jehovah Shalom** (the Lord is peace):

____

____

____

5. **Jehovah Rohi** (the Lord my shepherd):

____

____

____

6. **Jehovah Nissi** (the Lord my banner):

____

____

____

7. **Jehovah Rapha** (the Lord who heals):

____

____

____

8. **Jehovah Tsidkenu** (the Lord our righteousness):

____

____

____

9. **El Shaddai** (Lord God Almighty):

____

____

____

10. **Immanuel** (God with us):

____

____

____

Remember, God has a name for every situation you find yourself in. Whether you're feeling anxious or joyful or frustrated or excited, you can call on God, and He will always answer. He is so strong, so loving, so incredible, so awesome! And the best thing of all? He created you and longs to get to know you even more than you wish to know Him. So go ahead and cry out to Him, praise Him, confide in Him, and share everything with Him. He's more than the God of the universe—He's someone who has an amazing plan for your life and wants to walk with you every step of the way.

MORE GREAT HARVEST HOUSE BOOKS FOR KIDS

A Kid's Guide to the Armor of God

If you're between the ages of eight and twelve, you'll enjoy this helpful guide to the armor of God. Pastor and author Tony Evans shows you how to dress in the armor God provides so you'll able to speak the truth, stand firm in the faith, and spread the good news of Jesus.

The Awesome Book of Bible Answers for Kids

You probably have lots of important questions about Jesus, God, and faith. Respected Christian teacher Josh McDowell answers your questions straight from the Bible—in language that's easy to understand.

Bible Basics for Kids

In this fun, easy-to-read exploration of God, the Bible, and faith, kids like you can discover speedy summaries of every book of Scripture, a 90-day reading plan, memorization tricks, and more. Terry Glaspey and Kathleen Kerr make clear that the Bible is all about God reaching out to His children through Jesus.

How to Study Your Bible for Kids

One of America's best-loved Bible teachers shows kids like you how to study the Bible yourself in three steps—observation, interpretation, and application. You'll discover God's Word still applies today, and you'll better understand God's love for you.

To learn more about Harvest House books and to read sample chapters, visit our website:

www.harvesthousepublishers.com